Plant Based Diet For Weight Loss

Breakfast Recipes to Melt Fat!

Sidney Ellison

© **Copyright 2019 - All rights reserved.**

The contents of this book may not be reproduced, duplicated or transmitted without direct written permission from the author.

Under no circumstances will any legal responsibility or blame be held against the publisher for any reparation, damages, or monetary loss due to the information herein, either directly or indirectly.

Legal Notice:

This book is copyright protected. This is only for personal use. You cannot amend, distribute, sell, use, quote or paraphrase any part or the content within this book without the consent of the author.

Disclaimer Notice:

Please note the information contained within this document is for educational and entertainment purposes only. Every attempt has been made to provide accurate, up to date and reliable complete information. No warranties of any kind are expressed or implied. Readers acknowledge that the author is not engaging in the rendering of legal, financial, medical or professional advice. The content of this book has been derived from various sources. Please consult a licensed professional before attempting any techniques outlined in this book.

By reading this document, the reader agrees that under no circumstances is the author responsible for any losses, direct or indirect, which are incurred as a result of the use of information contained within this document, including, but not limited to, —errors, omissions, or inaccuracies.

Books by Sidney Ellison

Scan the Code to Learn More

Plant Based Diet Meal Plan- Delicious Recipes for Clean Eating

Plant Based Diet for Weight Loss- Breakfast Recipes to Melt Fat

Vegan Meal Prep- Zero Worry, Delicious Breakfast Recipes

Vegan Cookbook for Athletes: Lip Smacking Breakfast Recipes for High Performance

Bonus Offer: Get the Ebook absolutely free when you purchase the paperback via Kindle Matchbook!

Table of Contents

Introduction...1

Chapter One: A Plant-Based Diet..2

    Benefits of the plant-based diet:..5

    Foods to consume:...7

Chapter Two: Weight Loss Breakfast Smoothies.........................8

    Kiwi and Kale Smoothie.. 8

    Wake Up Smoothie..10

    Spinach, Avocado and Banana Smoothie......................... 11

    Piña Colada Smoothie.. 12

    The Glowing Green Smoothie.. 13

    Blueberry Protein Weight loss Breakfast Smoothie..........14

    Detox Smoothie... 15

    Berry n Beet Smoothie.. 16

    Breakfast Green Smoothie... 17

    Strawberry Pistachio Cream...18

    Eggnog Smoothie.. 19

    Mixed Berry and Fennel Smoothie................................... 20

    Dark Chocolate Banana Nut Smoothie............................22

Tabasco Cherry Smoothie 23

Fat Burning Smoothie 24

Ideal Weight Loss Smoothie 25

Beet N Beet Greens Smoothie 26

Spinach Flax Protein Smoothie 27

Pear Berry Weight-Loss Smoothie 28

Rock melon Soya and Flax Smoothie 29

Low Sugar Strawberry Smoothie 30

Chapter Three: Vegan Scrambles and Hash Recipes 31

Vegan Migas 31

Scrambled Tofu with Kale 34

Tofu Scramble with Bell Pepper and Mushrooms 36

Sweet Potato Hash Browns 37

Apple Sweet Potato Hash 38

Mixed Vegetable Hash 39

Potato, Asparagus & Mushroom Hash 43

Chapter Four: Breakfast Bowls 45

Pitaya Breakfast Bowl 45

Chia Yogurt Power Bowl 48

Chunky Monkey Breakfast Quinoa Bowl 49

Roasted Vegetable Bowls with Almond Butter Dressing . 52

Green Spring Vegetable Bowls & Creamy Chimichurri....55

Vanilla Quinoa and Roasted Blueberry Breakfast Bowl...57

Chapter Five: Plant Based Breakfast Cereals (Oats, Quinoa, Chia seeds etc.)..58

Quinoa & Chia Oatmeal Mix..58

Granola..60

Oat-Walnut Granola..61

Crunchy Granola Wedges..63

Fall Oatmeal Power Bowl...65

Chocolate Peanut Butter Protein Baked Oatmeal Cups...66

Roasted Banana Smash Oatmeal.......................................68

Banana Apple Porridge...69

Coconut Overnight Oatmeal..70

Flat-Belly Overnight Oats...71

Creamy Polenta...72

Pumpkin Pie Breakfast Sorghum..73

Dark Chocolate Pumpkin Oatmeal.....................................74

Three-Grain Porridge..75

Savory Curry Cashew Oatmeal...76

Breakfast Oatmeal Risotto...77

Crispy Quinoa Cakes..79

Vegetables & Creamy Polenta Recipe................................ 81

Chapter Six: Plant Based Breakfast Wrap, Burrito and Taco Recipes..82

Edamame IIummus Wrap.. 82

Greek Salad Wraps...83

Red Pepper, Goat Cheese, and Fresh Mint Wraps........... 85

Mexican Breakfast Burritos.. 87

Chipotle Bean Burritos... 89

Roasted Chickpea and Broccoli Burrito.............................91

Breakfast Tacos...93

Healthy Breakfast Tacos with Tofu & Roasted Potatoes..95

Black Bean and Tofu Breakfast Tostadas.........................97

Chapter Seven: Plant Based Breakfast Pudding and Parfait Recipes..99

Blackberry and Chia Breakfast Pudding........................... 99

Gingerbread Chia Pudding.. 100

Chocolate Chia Pudding with Raspberries...................... 101

Mango Coconut Chia Pudding..102

Orange Chia Pudding..103

Strawberry, Almond Butter and Oatmeal Breakfast Parfait104

Peach Pie Breakfast Parfait.. 105

Chapter Eight: Plant Based Breakfast Pancake, Waffle, Crepe and Omelet Recipes..106

    Vegan Pancakes.. 106

    Gingerbread Pancakes..108

    Chocolate Chip Banana Pancakes......................................110

    Crunchy Dill Chickpea Pancakes with Lemon-Garlic Aioli112

    Coconut Flour Pancakes...114

    Chive Waffles with Maple & Soy Mushrooms.................. 115

    Vegan Crepes...117

    Chocolate Coconut Crepes... 118

    Cinnamon Sugar Crepes...119

    Vegan Chickpea Omelette.. 120

    Lentil Veggie Asparagus Frittata....................................... 122

    Asparagus & Mushroom Vegan Quiche............................124

    Mexican Vegan Frittata..126

Chapter Nine: Plant Based Breakfast Toast and Sandwich Recipes.. 128

    Avocado and Feta Toast...128

    Banana French toast with Caramelized Bananas............129

    White Bean & Avocado Toast.. 131

    Mexi-Melt..132

    Peanut Butter-Banana Cinnamon Toast.......................... 133

Creamy Spinach Toast... 134

Masala Cheese Toast.. 136

Quark & Cucumber Toast... 138

Grilled Corn and Capsicum Sandwich................................. 139

Veggie Sandwich..140

Warm Goat Cheese, Beet and Arugula Sandwiches......... 141

Chapter Ten: Plant Based Breakfast Baking Recipes (Muffins, Breads, Scones, etc.)..143

Chocolate Muffins... 143

Cherry Dark Chocolate Chip Muffins................................. 145

Banana Nut Muffins... 147

Peanut Butter & Chia Berry Jam English Muffins.......... 148

Whole Wheat Bread... 149

Blueberry Mini Muffins... 151

Strawberry Banana Mini Bread Loaves / Muffins........... 153

Quinoa Flour Pumpkin Bread... 155

Pumpkin Bread.. 157

Banana Apple Chunk Bread... 159

Strawberry Breakfast Cake..160

Protein-Packed Breakfast Brownies..................................... 162

Pineapple Scones... 163

Garlicky Cheddar Biscuits with Sausage Gravy............166

Easy Pumpkin Spice Bagels..................................169

Chapter Eleven: Plant Based Breakfast Sausages...................171

Classic Breakfast Links..171

Chickpea Hemp Seed Sausages.................................173

Homemade Vegan Sausages......................................175

Vegetarian "Sausage" Patties..................................... 176

Vegan 'Bacon'... 178

Chapter Twelve: Plant Based Breakfast Recipes with Beans and Lentils... 179

Gigantes Plaki (Greek Baked Beans)..............................179

Sweet Potato, Chickpea, and Quinoa Veggie Burger.......181

Baked Beans... 183

Quick Breakfast Quinoa and Black Bean Vegan Chili.... 185

Veggie Vegan Breakfast Skillet................................... 187

Polenta and Beans.. 189

Breakfast Chickpeas with Cucumber..............................191

Chapter Thirteen: Plant Based Breakfast Casserole Recipes 192

Quinoa and Broccoli Casserole...................................192

Pumpkin Spice Latte Quinoa Breakfast Casserole..........195

Breakfast Hash Casserole with Butternut Squash & Cilantro..197

Sausage-Flavored Breakfast Beans and Grits ... 198

Chapter Fourteen: Plant Based Breakfast Soup Recipes ... 200

Turmeric Chickpea Vegetable Soup ... 200

Detox Breakfast Stew ... 202

Lemony Coconut Lentil Soup ... 206

Vegetarian Breakfast Posole ... 208

Chipotle Black Bean Tortilla Soup ... 210

Chapter Fifteen: Plant Based Breakfast Salad Recipes ... 212

Baby Kale Breakfast Salad with Quinoa & Strawberries 212

Pomegranate-Farro Breakfast Salad with Honey Ricotta 213

Coronation Chickpea and Apple Salad ... 214

Barley Salad with Tomatoes, Cucumber and Parsley ... 216

Three-Bean Salad ... 217

Chapter Sixteen: Plant Based Breakfast Recipes with Fruits 219

Whole Grain Peanut Butter and Fruit Toast ... 219

Morning Banana Split ... 221

Pineapple and Berry Salad ... 222

Grapefruit, Agave & Pistachio Salad ... 223

Fruit Punch ... 224

Papaya Boat Parfait ... 225

Healthy Breakfast Fruit Pizza ... 226

Summertime Fruit Salad..228

Blueberry-Pineapple Salad with Creamy Yogurt Dressing 229

Fresh Fruit Medley.. 230

Chapter Seventeen: Plant Based Breakfast Bar and Bites Recipes.. 231

Chocolate Peanut Butter Oatmeal Bars............................231

Cheesecake Breakfast Bars... 233

Strawberry Rhubarb Buckwheat Bars............................234

Peanut Butter Breakfast Bar...236

Apricot Oats Protein Bars..237

Cranberry Blueberry Crumb Bars..................................239

Black Bean Brownie Bites...241

Key Lime Pie Energy Bites.. 243

Banana-Oat Protein Balls... 244

Conclusion...245

Introduction

The modern-day diet and lifestyle have strayed a lot from the healthy lifestyle that our ancestors led. Food is a necessity for good health, but not all food is good food. What you eat has a significant impact on your body and overall health. You may have tried a lot of diets thinking they are healthy as well. However, most of the popular diets are just fad diets that do nothing good for your health and may even affect you negatively.

This is where the plant-based diet is different and can help you. This book will help you learn how the plant-based diet can benefit your health and how to follow it. Numerous recipes will help you apply this diet to your daily life. The focus of this book is on breakfast recipes from a plant-based diet. As you try out all the different breakfast recipes in this book, you will see that the diet is not hard to follow at all.

Although this book is focused on breakfast recipes, it is just one part of a series of other plant-based recipe books. These recipes will help you make deliciously healthy meals for any time of the day. But for now, a healthy breakfast is a good place to begin with. Learn a little about the plant-based diet and then get started on trying all the yummy recipes in the book.

Chapter One: A Plant-Based Diet

Before you begin following the plant-based diet, you should understand what it is and why you should follow it in the first place. As you read this, you will realize just how beneficial this diet can be for your health.

A plant-based diet is exactly what it sounds like. This means that you will only be eating foods that are derived from plant sources, and no animal foods are allowed. It may sound impossible or completely unappealing at first, but you will soon understand the value of such a diet and why we recommend it. When you follow the plant-based diet, you need to abstain from consuming anything that is derived from animal sources and this includes meat, eggs and even dairy if you can. Giving up these foods will not be much of a sacrifice because plant-based foods are also available in a large variety. Giving up animal foods will not mean that you have monotonous and tasteless meals at all. In fact, there are millions of people who have been following this kind of plant-based diet all their lives and are totally satisfied with it.

Not only is this diet good for your health, but it is also an environmentally conscious decision that you will be committing to. It will make you a conscious consumer as you take more notice of what you buy or eat in the future. Most of us just pick up anything we like at the grocery store without paying attention to the exact ingredients in those foods. Most of the processed foods we consume are filled with harmful preservatives, hidden sugars, and other unhealthy ingredients. But when you commit to the plant-based diet, you have to check that no animal sourced ingredients are included in your foods. This will give you a chance to take notice of everything that you will be consuming, and this is one of the best things you can do for your health. The food industry has compromised on the common man's health for their own profit. However, it is time to pay attention and take control of your own health again. This means you have to stop eating unhealthy foods that do not benefit your health. Animal foods are not always the same as processed factory-produced food, but the plant-based diet is still a better alternative.

It is better to eat as much organic food as possible and less of other types of food that are subjected to a lot of processing and chemicals. The plant-based diet can be followed in a few different ways. Different people have a different approach to this diet, and you can choose your own way as well. For instance, you may decide to go all the way and cut off every single animal product, including dairy. However, some people stop eating meat but still consume milk, eggs, etc.

The following are some of the basic principles of the plant-based diet to guide you:

- Consumption of animal products should be omitted or limited.

- Reduce consumption of any highly processed foods and consume only minimally processed or whole natural foods.

- The majority of food consumed should be sourced from plants. This means more vegetables, fruits, legumes, whole grains, nuts and seeds.

- Refined foods like sugar, refined oils, etc. should not be consumed.

- Try to source more organic and locally produced food to ensure better quality.

Although it may seem like the diet is the same as a vegan or even a vegetarian diet, it is not. These diets are similar in many ways but also have their differences. Hence it would be incorrect to use the term plant-based diet interchangeably with a vegan diet or vegetarian diet. A vegan will not eat any animal-sourced food like milk, meat, eggs, seafood, honey, or poultry. A vegetarian will not eat meat or poultry but may consume dairy products like milk or eggs. As opposed to these two diets, the plant-based diet is a lot more flexible. This is why it is easier to switch to this diet for most people.

As we already mentioned, the plant-based diet is environmentally conscious. It is also extremely healthy for you, and an added bonus is that it helps you lose unwanted weight. Most people look toward diets to help them lose weight. However, they often fail to find a healthy way to do this and opt for fad diets that claim to help you lose 10 pounds in a week. You have to understand that this kind of approach is usually very unhealthy and the weight loss will not even be long term. The plant-based diet can help you lose weight by eating less junk food and other unhealthy foods. It will facilitate a better digestive system and help you maintain a healthier weight. So for those who are looking for a weight loss solution, this diet is definitely a good option. It will show slower results, but weight loss will be healthy and can be maintained in the long term.

A lot of people shy away from the plant-based diet, thinking that it is very restrictive. In truth, this diet is very flexible, and the amounts of plant-based foods available are a lot more than you could possibly imagine. You might be giving up meat, but there are so many more plant varieties in the world than there are animals. There are thousands of different recipes you can try from around the world to help you utilize these plant-based ingredients and cook deliciously healthy meals. All the varieties of vegetables, fruits, legumes, etc. can be used to make many different kinds of dishes every single day. This is why it would be unfair to assume or claim that the plant-based diet is restrictive and hard to follow.

Benefits of the plant-based diet:

As you read about the plant-based diet, you may still be seeking more clarity on exactly how it is beneficial for you to follow this diet. This section will help you understand the various benefits of the plant-based diet.

It will help you lose weight.

More than half of the current population suffers from obesity and other weight issues. This is mainly due to the excessive consumption of junk food or highly processed foods and too much sugar. Many studies have shown that switching to a plant-based diet helps people lose excess weight, and it also helps them keep the weight off in the long term.

It is a heart-healthy diet.

Depending on how you follow this diet, it can help you improve your heart health a lot. Eating more fruit, vegetables, nuts and legumes is much better for your heart than consuming a lot of red meat, refined grains, or sugary beverages. Eating good food will help in the prevention of heart diseases.

It reduces the risk of cancer.

A lot of research shows that those who follow a plant-based diet have a lower risk of suffering from certain types of cancer. This is especially so in the case of gastrointestinal cancer and colorectal cancer. Those who eat fish with this diet and stop eating meat are actually at a higher advantage than others.

It protects against cognitive decline.

Studies show that a diet rich in plant-based foods can help to lower the risk or development of cognitive decline. The high amount of antioxidants in such foods and other plant compounds can even lower the progression of diseases like Alzheimer's. It will also reduce the risk of developing dementia or other cognitive impairments.

It helps in the prevention and control of diabetes.

People who eat more plant-based foods are at a much lower risk of developing diabetes compared to others who follow a more unhealthy type of diet. This type of diet has also helped people to control their blood sugar levels in a healthier manner.

A plant-based diet is better for the planet.

Other than the personal health benefits of this diet, you should also appreciate its positive impact on the environment. The environmental footprint of a plant-based diet is much smaller than that of a carnivorous diet. If you adopt sustainable eating habits, it will help to lower environmental degradation and global warming. The western diet results in a lot of gas emissions and causes a lot of water wastage as well.

These are some of the many benefits of the plant-based diet.

Foods to consume:

The following are the foods that you should eat more of when you commit to the plant-based diet.

- Vegetables. This includes spinach, kale, cauliflower, potatoes, broccoli, asparagus and tons of different vegetables.
- Fruit. This includes peaches, pears, oranges, berries, bananas, mango and others.
- Whole grains. These are a better alternative than refined grains that are harmful to health. This includes quinoa, brown rice, barley, rolled oats, etc.
- Legumes. These include black beans, chickpeas, peas, lentils, etc. and are great for health.
- Seeds and nuts. These include sunflower seeds, cashew nuts, peanuts, pumpkin seeds and others. Making homemade butter from these are also a great option.
- Plant-based milk. Instead of animal milk, you can have almond milk, soymilk, coconut milk and cashew milk.
- Spices and herbs. These include rosemary, dill, turmeric, basil, black pepper, etc.
- Beverages include water, herbal teas, fresh juices and no added sugars in these.

Chapter Two: Weight Loss Breakfast Smoothies

Kiwi and Kale Smoothie

Number of servings: 1

Nutritional values per serving:

Calories – 174, Fat – 5 g, Carbohydrate – 24 g, Fiber – 3 g, Protein – 11 g

Ingredients:

- ¾ cup skim milk
- ½ kiwifruit, peeled, chopped
- ½ teaspoon agave nectar, honey or maple syrup
- 1 cup torn kale (discard hard stems and ribs)
- ½ tablespoon smooth peanut butter, unsalted

Directions

1. Gather all the ingredients and add into a blender.
2. Blend for 30 to 40 seconds or until smooth and creamy.
3. Pour into a glass and serve with crushed ice.

Wake Up Smoothie

Number of servings: 6

Nutritional values per serving: 1 cup, without sweetener

Calories – 139, Fat – 2 g, Carbohydrate – 33 g, Fiber – 4 g, Protein – 2.6 g

Ingredients:

- 2 bananas, peeled, sliced
- 1 cup low- fat silken tofu or low- fat plain yogurt
- 2 ½ cups orange juice
- 2 ½ cups frozen berries of your choice
- Sweetener to taste of your choice (optional)

Directions:

1. Gather all the ingredients and add into a blender.
2. Blend for 30 to 40 seconds or until smooth and creamy.
3. Pour into 6 glasses and serve.

Spinach, Avocado and Banana Smoothie

Number of servings: 1

Nutritional values per serving:

Calories – 215, Fat – 8 g, Carbohydrate – 22 g, Fiber – 7 g, Protein – 13 g

Ingredients:

- 1 small banana, sliced
- ¼ avocado, peeled, chopped
- A handful spinach, torn
- 1 scoop plant based protein powder
- 1 cup almond milk, unsweetened
- ½ tablespoon MCT oil

Directions

1. Gather all the ingredients and add into a blender.
2. Blend for 30 to 40 seconds or until smooth and creamy.
3. Pour into a glass and serve.

Piña Colada Smoothie

Number of servings: 2

Nutritional values per serving:

Calories – 143, Fat – 3.8 g, Carbohydrate – 29.5 g, Fiber – 3.1 g, Protein – 2 g

Ingredients:

- 1 ½ cups fresh pineapple chunks
- 1 small banana, sliced
- 2 inches lemongrass, minced
- ½ cup light coconut milk
- 2 teaspoons coconut flakes, unsweetened
- Ice cubes, as required

Directions:

1. Gather all the ingredients and add into a blender.
2. Blend for 30 to 40 seconds or until smooth and creamy.
3. Pour into 2 glasses and serve.

The Glowing Green Smoothie

Number of servings: 4

Nutritional values per serving:

Calories – 154, Fat – 1.1 g, Carbohydrate – 36.7 g, Fiber – 10.5 g, Protein – 5.1 g

Ingredients:

- 2 heads Romaine lettuce, torn
- 1 large bunch spinach, chopped
- 2 pears, cored, chopped
- 2 apples, cored, chopped
- 2 bananas, sliced
- 7-8 stalks celery, chopped
- Juice of a lemon
- 3 cups water
- 1 cup chopped fresh cilantro or parsley (optional)

Directions:

1. Gather all the ingredients and add into a blender.
2. Blend for 30 to 40 seconds or until smooth and creamy.
3. Pour into 4 glasses and serve.

Blueberry Protein Weight loss Breakfast Smoothie

Number of servings: 2

Nutritional values per serving:

Calories – 224, Fat – 4 g, Carbohydrate – 19 g, Fiber – 4 g, Protein – 20 g

Ingredients:

- 1 cup frozen blueberries
- 1 cup vanilla almond milk, unsweetened
- 1 teaspoon fresh lemon juice
- 1 tablespoon almond butter
- 2 scoops vanilla plant based protein powder
- Water, as required

Directions:

1. Gather all the ingredients and add into a blender.
2. Blend for 30 to 40 seconds or until smooth and creamy.
3. Pour into 2 glasses and serve.

Detox Smoothie

Number of servings: 2

Nutritional values per serving:

Calories – 236, Fat – 6.5g, Carbohydrate – 44.8 g, Fiber – 10 g, Protein – 4.7 g

Ingredients:

- 2 cups chopped spinach
- ½ cup mashed avocado
- 2 bananas, sliced, frozen
- 2 cups coconut water
- 4 tablespoons fresh lemon juice
- 2 tablespoons aloe Vera juice
- 1/8 teaspoon cayenne pepper or more to taste
- Few coconut water ice cubes

Directions:

1. Pour some coconut water into an ice tray. Freeze until firm. Use these coconut water ice cubes.
2. Gather all the ingredients and add into a blender.
3. Blend for 30 to 40 seconds or until smooth and creamy.
4. Pour into 2 glasses and serve.

Berry n Beet Smoothie

Number of servings: 1

Nutritional values per serving:

Calories – 146, Fat – 3.7 g, Carbohydrate – 27.8 g, Fiber – NA, Protein – 3 g

Ingredients:

- ½ small beet
- ½ cup frozen mixed berries
- 2 bananas, sliced, frozen
- 2 cups chopped spinach
- 3 cups almond milk, unsweetened
- 2 teaspoons chia seeds
- ½ teaspoon vanilla extract

Directions:

1. Slice the banana and place on a cookie sheet. Place cookie sheet in the freezer until banana is frozen.
2. Boil the beet in a small pot of water. Drain and cool. Peel and chop into pieces.
3. Gather all the ingredients and add into a blender.
4. Blend for 30-40 seconds until smooth.
5. Pour into tall glasses and serve.

Breakfast Green Smoothie

Number of servings: 4

Nutritional values per serving:

Calories – 104, Fat – 0.5 g, Carbohydrate – 25.5 g, Fiber – 7.1 g, Protein – 2.5 g

Ingredients:

- 4 cups chopped spinach
- 6 stalks celery, chopped
- 6 carrots, chopped
- 1 orange, separated into segments, deseeded
- ½ lemon, peeled, deseeded
- ½ pineapple, peeled, chopped into chunks
- 1 cucumber, chopped, deseeded
- 1 bunch parsley, chopped
- 4 apples, cored, chopped
- ½ lime, peeled, deseeded
- 2 bunches fresh mint, chopped

Directions:

1. Gather all the ingredients and add into a blender.
2. Blend for 30 to 40 seconds or until smooth and creamy.
3. Pour into 4 glasses and serve.

Strawberry Pistachio Cream

Number of servings: 2

Nutritional values per serving:

Calories – 266, Fat – 9 g, Carbohydrate – 18 g, Fiber – 5 g, Protein – 30 g

Ingredients:

- 2 cups frozen strawberries
- 1 avocado, peeled, pitted, chopped
- ½ cup pistachios
- ½ teaspoon vanilla extract
- Water, as required
- 2 teaspoons vanilla extract
- Ice cubes, as required

Directions:

1. Gather all the ingredients and add into a blender.
2. Blend for 30 to 40 seconds or until smooth and creamy.
3. Pour into 2 glasses and serve.

Eggnog Smoothie

Number of servings: 1

Nutritional values per serving:

Calories – 145, Fat – 5.7 g, Carbohydrate – 23.3 g, Fiber – 3.8 g, Protein – 2.4 g

Ingredients:

- 1 ½ cups almond milk
- 1 teaspoon ground nutmeg
- 4 dates, pitted, chopped
- 2 bananas, sliced
- 2 teaspoons almond extract

Directions:

1. Gather all the ingredients and add into a blender.
2. Blend for 30 to 40 seconds or until smooth and creamy.
3. Pour into a glass and serve.

Mixed Berry and Fennel Smoothie

Number of servings: 2

Nutritional values per serving:

Calories – 55, Fat – 3.1 g, Carbohydrate – 12.8 g, Fiber – 4.6 g, Protein – 2.1 g

Ingredients:

- 1 cup mixed berries
- 1 cup almond milk
- 4 medium fennel bulbs, shredded
- 2 tablespoons sunflower seeds

Directions:

1. Gather all the ingredients and add into a blender.
2. Blend for 30 to 40 seconds or until smooth and creamy.
3. Pour into 2 glasses and serve.

Peach Oat Cobbler Smoothie

Number of servings: 2

Nutritional values per serving:

Calories – 277, Fat – 4 g, Carbohydrate – 33 g, Fiber – 6 g, Protein – 28 g

Ingredients:

- 1 peach, pitted, chopped
- 1 cup almond milk, unsweetened
- 2 scoops plant based vanilla protein powder
- 1 banana, sliced, frozen
- 1 cup almond milk, unsweetened
- 4 tablespoons rolled oats
- 2 teaspoons ground flaxseeds

Directions:

1. Gather all the ingredients and add into a blender.
2. Blend for 30 to 40 seconds or until smooth and creamy.
3. Pour into a glass and serve.

Dark Chocolate Banana Nut Smoothie

Number of servings: 2

Nutritional values per serving:

Calories – 229, Fat – 11 g, Carbohydrate – 26 g, Fiber – 7 g, Protein – 28 g

Ingredients:

- 1 banana, sliced
- 2 cups almond milk, unsweetened
- Ice cubes, as required
- Water, as required
- 2 teaspoons dark chocolate morsels
- ¼ cup chopped walnuts
- 2/3 cup chocolate plant based protein powder

Directions:

1. Gather all the ingredients and add into a blender.
2. Blend for 30 to 40 seconds or until smooth and creamy.
3. Pour into 2 glasses and serve.

Tabasco Cherry Smoothie

Number of servings: 2

Nutritional values per serving:

Calories – 232, Fat – 2g, Carbohydrate – 28 g, Fiber – 3.5 g, Protein – 26 g

Ingredients:

- 1 banana, sliced, frozen
- 1 cup cherries, pitted
- 2 teaspoons Tabasco sauce
- ½ cup almond milk, unsweetened
- Ice cubes, as required
- Juice of ½ lime
- 2 scoops plant based plain protein powder
- Water, as required

Directions:

1. Gather all the ingredients and add into a blender.
2. Blend for 30 to 40 seconds or until smooth and creamy.
3. Pour into 2 glasses and serve.

Fat Burning Smoothie

Number of servings: 1

Nutritional values per serving:

Calories – 215, Fat – 8.3 g, Carbohydrate – 37 g, Fiber – 5.4 g, Protein – 4.4 g

Ingredients:

- 1 cup chopped spinach
- 1 stalk celery, chopped
- ½ large grapefruit, peeled, separated into segments, deseeded
- 1 small avocado, peeled, pitted, chopped
- A handful fresh mint leaves
- ½ cup brewed green tea, cooled
- 1 cup frozen pineapple chunks
- A pinch cayenne pepper powder (optional)

Directions:

1. Gather all the ingredients and add into a blender.
2. Blend for 30 to 40 seconds or until smooth and creamy.
3. Pour into a glass and serve.

Ideal Weight Loss Smoothie

Number of servings: 2

Nutritional values per serving:

Calories – 331, Fat – 24 g, Carbohydrate – 31 g, Fiber – 11 g, Protein – 4 g

Ingredients:

- 1 medium avocado
- 2 cups water
- 2 tablespoons chia seeds
- 1 cup blueberries, fresh or frozen
- 1 tablespoon coconut oil
- 1 tablespoon honey or stevia drops (optional)
- ½ teaspoon cinnamon powder

Directions:

1. Gather all the ingredients and add into a blender.
2. Blend until smooth.
3. Pour into 2 glasses and serve with crushed ice if desired.
4. During the first week add only half tablespoon of coconut oil per smoothie. You can gradually increase it to a tablespoon per smoothie after a week.

Beet N Beet Greens Smoothie

Number of servings: 2

Nutritional values per serving:

Calories – 84, Fat – 1.5 g, Carbohydrate – 18 g, Fiber – 4 g, Protein – 2 g

Ingredients:

- ¾ cup almond milk, unsweetened
- 1 cup beet greens, discard hard stems, chopped
- 3.5 ounces raw beets, peeled chopped
- Juice of half an orange
- ¾ cup mixed berries, frozen
- 1 small banana, sliced, frozen

Directions:

1. Gather all the ingredients and add into a blender.
2. Blend for 30 to 40 seconds or until smooth and creamy.
3. Pour into 2 glasses and serve.

Spinach Flax Protein Smoothie

Number of servings: 2

Nutritional values per serving: Large smoothie

Calories – 231, Fat – 8 g, Carbohydrate – 23 g, Fiber – 9 g, Protein – 19 g

Ingredients:

- 2 cups almond milk, unsweetened
- ½ cup frozen mango chunks
- 1 banana, peeled, sliced
- ½ cup frozen pineapple pieces
- 2 tablespoons chia seeds (optional)
- 2 tablespoons flax meal (optional)
- 2 cups baby spinach
- 2 scoops vanilla protein powder

Directions:

1. Gather all the ingredients and add all the ingredients into a blender.
2. Blend until smooth and creamy.
3. Pour into 2 glasses and serve.
4. Serve with crushed ice.

Pear Berry Weight-Loss Smoothie

Number of servings: 4

Nutritional values per serving: large serving

Calories – 354, Fat – 9.3 g, Carbohydrate – 61.6 g, Fiber – 19 g, Protein – 13 g

Ingredients:

- 2 pears, cored, peeled, chopped
- ½ ripe avocado, peeled, pitted, chopped
- 2 cups torn spinach
- 2 kiwifruits, peeled, chopped
- 2 cups frozen raspberries
- 6 ounces nonfat vanilla Greek yogurt
- 4 cups cold water

Directions:

1. Gather all the ingredients and add into a blender and blend until smooth.
2. Pour into 4 glasses and serve.
3. Serve with crushed ice.

Rock melon Soya and Flax Smoothie

Number of servings: 2

Nutritional values per serving: large serving

Calories – 105, Fat – 2.9 g, Carbohydrate – 14.6 g, Fiber – 1.9 g, Protein – 5.0 g

Ingredients:

- 1 cup diced rock melon + extra to garnish
- 1 tablespoon flaxseeds
- 1 cup soy milk
- ½ cup crushed ice, to serve (optional)

Directions:

1. Add all the ingredients into a blender and blend until smooth.
2. Pour into 2 glasses and serve garnished with slices of rock melon.
3. Serve with crushed ice if desired.

Low Sugar Strawberry Smoothie

Number of servings: 4

Nutritional values per serving: 1 cup

Calories – 350, Fat – 11 g, Carbohydrate – 42 g, Fiber – 14 g, Protein – 22 g

Ingredients:

- 2 cups chopped spinach
- 10 strawberries + strawberry slices to garnish
- 2/3 cup cooked oats
- ½ cup plain Greek yogurt
- 2 tablespoons chia seeds
- 2 cups soy milk
- Stevia to taste

Directions:

1. Gather all the ingredients and add into a blender.
2. Blend until smooth and creamy.
3. Pour into tall glasses.
4. Garnish with slices of strawberry and serve with crushed ice.

Chapter Three: Vegan Scrambles and Hash Recipes

Vegan Migas

Number of servings: 2

Nutritional values per serving:

Calories – 334, Fat – 14 g, Carbohydrate – 42 g, Fiber – 7 g, Protein – 14 g

Ingredients:

For Salsa Ranchera:

- 3 large ripe tomatoes
- 1-2 jalapeno or Serrano chilies
- 4 cloves garlic, unpeeled
- ¼ teaspoon salt
- 1 tablespoon canola oil or sunflower oil

For Vegan Migas:

- ½ package (from a 14 ounces package) soft tofu, drained, pressed of excess moisture, crumbled
- 1 ½ stale corn tortillas, cut into strips
- 3 jalapeno or Serrano chilies, finely chopped, deseed if desired
- Salt to taste
- 1 plum tomato, diced
- 1 tablespoon canola oil, divided
- 1/8 teaspoon ground turmeric
- 2 scallions, trimmed, chopped
- ¼ teaspoon ground chipotle chili
- ¼ cup shredded non-dairy cheese

- 4 corn tortillas, warmed according to the instructions on the package
- A handful fresh cilantro, chopped

Directions:

1. To make Salsa Ranchera: Place a cast iron skillet over medium heat. Add tomatoes, garlic and chilies. Cook until the skin of the tomato, chili and garlic are charred. Turn the tomatoes, garlic and chilies in between a few times. Remove them one by one as they get charred and place on a plate. Let it cool for a few minutes.
2. Peel the garlic and add into a blender. Also add the charred tomato and chilies. Blend the ingredients until smooth.
3. Place the skillet back over medium heat. Add oil. When oil is heated, add the blended mixture. Add salt and mix well. Cook until the mixture is thick.
4. Remove from heat and transfer into a bowl. Cover and set aside. Use as much as required and refrigerate the rest for the next time or for any other recipe.
5. To make Vegan Migas: Place a nonstick skillet over medium flame. Add ½ teaspoon oil. Swirl the pan to spread the oil. Add tortilla strips and cook until the underside is crisp and golden in color. Turn the strips and cook until crisp. Remove from the skillet and set aside on a plate.
6. Place the pan back on heat. Add the remaining oil. When oil is heated, add tofu and sauté for a couple of minutes.
7. Add turmeric, chilies, chipotle chili powder, scallions and salt. Stir frequently and cook until nearly dry.
8. Add cilantro, cheese, tomatoes and the crisp tortillas strips. Sauté for a couple of minutes until the cheese melts.

9. To serve: Place 2 tortillas in each plate. Divide the tofu mixture among the tortillas. Serve about ¼ cup of Salsa Ranchera in each of the plates.

Scrambled Tofu with Kale

Number of servings: 2

Nutritional values per serving:

Calories – 210, Fat – 7g, Carbohydrate – 21 g, Fiber – 4.7 g, Protein – 20.6 g

Ingredients:

- 1 tablespoon extra-virgin olive oil
- 1 small red bell pepper, chopped
- 1 clove garlic, minced
- Freshly ground pepper to taste
- Kosher salt to taste
- ½ package (from a 14 ounces package) firm or extra - firm tofu, pressed of excess moisture, crumbled
- 2 tablespoons nutritional yeast
- 4 ounces mushrooms, sliced
- ½ teaspoon ground cumin
- ¾ -1 teaspoon smoked paprika
- ½ bunch kale (about 6 ounces), discard hard stems and ribs, chopped

Directions:

1. Place a skillet or wok over medium-high flame. Add oil. When the oil is heated, add red pepper and cook for a minute.
2. Add garlic and sauté until fragrant. Add mushroom, salt and pepper. Sauté for a couple of minutes.
3. Add tofu and heat thoroughly.
4. Lower the heat to medium heat. Add kale and mix well. Sprinkle some water if desired.
5. Cover and cook until kale is tender. Stir frequently.

6. Stir in nutritional yeast, salt and pepper. Cook for a couple of minutes and serve.

Tofu Scramble with Bell Pepper and Mushrooms

Number of servings: 1

Nutritional values per serving:

Calories – 134, Fat – 6 g, Carbohydrate – 7 g, Fiber – 1 g, Protein – 12 g

Ingredients:

- ½ cup + 2 tablespoons firm tofu, pressed of excess moisture, crumbled
- ¼ red bell pepper, diced
- ½ cup sliced mushrooms
- Salt to taste
- ¼ teaspoon Himalayan pink salt
- Pepper to taste
- 1/8 teaspoon turmeric powder
- ½ teaspoon canola oil
- Chopped parsley to garnish

Directions:

1. Place a skillet over medium heat. Add bell pepper, mushroom and about ¼ teaspoon salt and stir. Cook until tender. Push the vegetables to one side of the skillet.
2. Add oil in the center of the pan. When the oil heats, add tofu, turmeric pepper and black salt and sauté for a few minutes. Stir frequently.
3. Taste and adjust the seasonings if necessary.
4. Garnish with parsley and serve.

Sweet Potato Hash Browns

Number of servings: 3

Nutritional values per serving: 1 hash brown

Calories – 103, Fat – 7g, Carbohydrate – 9 g, Fiber – 1 g, Protein – 1 g

Ingredients:

- 2 ½ cups peeled, shredded sweet potatoes
- 2 small cloves garlic, peeled, grated
- ¼ teaspoon salt or to taste
- 2 tablespoons minced shallot
- 1 ½ tablespoons extra-virgin olive oil, divided
- ¼ teaspoon pepper or to taste

Directions:

1. Add ½ tablespoon oil and rest of the ingredients into a bowl and mix well.
2. Divide the mixture into 3 equal portions and shape into patties.
3. Place a cast-iron skillet or any other pan over medium-high heat. Add remaining oil. When the oil is heated, swirl the pan.
4. Lower the heat to medium-low and place the hash brown patties in it.
5. Cook until the underside is golden brown. Flip sides and cook the other side until golden brown.
6. Remove with a slotted spoon and place on a plate lined with paper towels.
7. Serve hot.

Apple Sweet Potato Hash

Number of servings: 2

Nutritional values per serving: Without hemp hearts

Calories – 97, Fat – 1 g, Carbohydrate – 19 g, Fiber – 3 g, Protein – 1 g

Ingredients:

- 1 large sweet potato, cubed
- 1 teaspoon coconut oil
- 1 small apple, cored, peeled, chopped
- ½ tablespoon chopped sage
- ¼ teaspoon salt
- ¼ teaspoon garlic powder
- Pepper to taste
- Hemp hearts to serve (optional)

Directions:

1. Place a skillet over medium heat. Add oil and let it melt.
2. Add apples, sage and sweet potato and mix well. Cook until sweet potatoes are tender.
3. Season with salt and pepper. Cook until sweet potatoes are soft.
4. Divide into plates and serve with hemp hearts if desired.

Mixed Vegetable Hash

Number of servings: 2-3

Nutritional values per serving: 1 cup

Calories – 120, Fat – 3.5 g, Carbohydrate – 21 g, Fiber – 3 g, Protein – 3.5 g

Ingredients:

- 6 ounces small new potatoes, unpeeled
- ½ teaspoon chopped fresh rosemary, divided
- 1 cup shredded broccoli
- 1 shallot, minced
- 3 tablespoons chopped red bell pepper
- 3 tablespoons chopped green bell pepper
- ½ small acorn squash, peeled, cubed (¼ inch cubes)
- Salt to taste
- Olive oil cooking spray
- Freshly ground pepper, to taste
- 1 teaspoon fresh lemon juice
- 2 teaspoons olive oil, divided

Directions:

1. Spray a baking dish with cooking spray. Place potatoes and squash in the baking dish. Sprinkle 1-teaspoon oil, salt, pepper and half the rosemary over it. Toss well and spread it evenly in the dish.
2. Roast in a preheated oven at 425°F for about 25-35 minutes until tender. Stir a couple of times while roasting.
3. Place a nonstick skillet over medium-high heat. Add 1-teaspoon oil. When the oil is heated, add shallot, all the bell peppers and broccoli and stir- fry for a minute.
4. Stir in the potato mixture and heat thoroughly.

5. Add rest of the ingredients and stir-fry for a couple of minutes.
6. Divide into plates and serve.

Hash Brown Potato Cakes

Number of servings: 4

Nutritional values per serving: 1 cake

Calories – 59, Fat – 2 g, Carbohydrate – 9 g, Fiber – 1 g, Protein – 1 g

Ingredients:

- 1 pound russet or round red potatoes, peeled, shredded
- ½ tablespoon olive oil
- Salt or to taste
- 1 small onion, quartered, thinly sliced
- 1 teaspoon snipped fresh thyme or ¼ teaspoon dried, crushed thyme
- Freshly ground black pepper
- Cooking spray

Directions:

1. Place potatoes in a colander. Rinse potatoes in cold water immediately after it is shredded. Let it sit in the colander for 15 minutes. Press lightly and place on paper towels to dry. Transfer into a bowl.
2. Add onion, oil, thyme, salt and pepper into the bowl of potatoes.
3. Place a nonstick skillet over medium heat. Spray with cooking spray.
4. Place ¼ of the mixture on the skillet. Press the mixture slightly with a spatula. Place 2-3 more similar cakes on the skillet.
5. Cook until the underside is golden brown. Flip sides. Cook the other side until golden brown.

6. When done, transfer on to a baking sheet to keep warm or serve immediately.

Potato, Asparagus & Mushroom Hash

Number of servings: 2

Nutritional values per serving: 1-¼ cups

Calories – 239, Fat – 11 g, Carbohydrate – 29 g, Fiber – 4 g, Protein – 5 g

Ingredients:

- ½ pound new or baby potatoes, scrubbed, cut into 2 halves if large in size
- ½ pound asparagus, trimmed, cut into ½ inch pieces
- ½ shallot, minced
- ½ small onion, chopped
- ¼ teaspoon salt or to taste
- A handful fresh chives, chopped to garnish
- 1 ½ tablespoons extra-virgin olive oil, divided
- 2 ounces shiitake mushroom caps or other mushrooms, sliced
- 1 small clove garlic, peeled, minced
- ½ tablespoon minced fresh sage
- ¼ cup roasted red pepper (from jar), sliced
- Freshly ground pepper to taste

Directions:

1. Place a pot with water (about 1 ½ inches from the bottom of the pot) over medium heat. Place a steamer basket in it. Place the potatoes in it and cover with a lid. Cook until just tender. It should not be over cooked.
2. Drain the potatoes and place on your cutting board. When cool enough to handle, cut into ½ inch pieces.
3. Place a nonstick pan over medium heat. Add ½ tablespoon oil. When the oil is heated, add shallot,

asparagus, garlic and mushrooms and cook until light brown. Transfer on to a plate.
4. Place the pan back over heat. Add remaining oil. When the oil is heated, add onion and potato and cook until brown. Scrape the bottom of the pan to remove any browned bits that may be stuck.
5. Add the vegetable mixture into the pan. Also add roasted red pepper, salt, pepper and sage and mix well. Heat thoroughly.
6. Garnish with chives and serve.

Chapter Four: Breakfast Bowls

Pitaya Breakfast Bowl

Serves: 1

Ingredients:

For smoothie:

- ½ cup package frozen or fresh Pitaya puree (Dragon fruit)
- 2 strawberries, sliced
- 2 tablespoons chia seeds
- 1/3 cup frozen pineapple chunks
- A pinch salt
- ½ tablespoon light agave nectar
- 1 tablespoon toasted unsweetened shredded coconut
- ¼ banana, sliccd
- 1 tablespoon toasted unsalted pistachio nuts

Directions:

1. Add pineapple, half the Pitaya, salt and agave nectar into a blender and blend until smooth.
2. Pour into a bowl. Add chia seeds and mix well.
3. Refrigerate for at least 15-30 minutes.
4. Top with banana and strawberry slices. Garnish with coconut and pistachio nuts and serve.

Cantaloupe Smoothie Bowl

Number of servings: 1

Nutritional values per serving:

Calories – 135, Fat – 1 g, Carbohydrate – 32 g, Fiber – 3 g, Protein – 3 g

Ingredients:

For smoothie:

- 2 cups cubed, frozen cantaloupe
- A wee bit salt
- 6 tablespoons fresh carrot juice

For topping:

- A handful melon balls
- 1 tablespoon chopped nuts
- A handful berries of your choice
- 2-3 basil leaves, torn

Directions:

1. Add all the ingredients for smoothie into a blender and blend until smooth.
2. Pour into a bowl.
3. Place toppings on top and serve.

Chia Yogurt Power Bowl

Number of servings: 3

Nutritional values per serving:

Calories – 103, Fat – 3 g, Carbohydrate – 15 g, Fiber – 3 g, Protein – 10 g

Ingredients:

For yogurt bowl:

- 1 cup nonfat Greek yogurt
- 2 tablespoons chia seeds
- 1 ½ tablespoons honey or agave nectar or maple syrup
- ¾ cup milk of your choice
- 1 teaspoon vanilla extract

For topping:

- A handful blueberries
- 1 teaspoon chia seeds
- 3 teaspoons pecans
- ½ teaspoon grated lemon zest

Directions:

1. Add all the ingredients for yogurt bowl into a mixing bowl. Whisk well.
2. Chill for 4-8 hours.
3. Divide into 3 bowls.
4. Divide the toppings among the bowls and serve.

Chunky Monkey Breakfast Quinoa Bowl

Number of servings: 2

Nutritional values per serving: Without toppings

Calories – 292, Fat – 9 g, Carbohydrate – 44 g, Fiber – 5 g, Protein – 10 g

Ingredients:

- ½ cup quinoa, rinsed, drained
- Salt to taste
- 1 medium size ripe banana, mashed
- 1 ½ tablespoons cocoa powder
- 1 cup water
- 6 tablespoons non-dairy milk of your choice
- 2 tablespoons peanut butter
- 1 ½ tablespoons maple syrup

Directions:

1. Add water into a pot. Place the pot over high heat. When the water begins to boil, lower the heat to low heat and add quinoa and salt. Cover and cook until dry.
2. Add rest of the ingredients and stir. Heat thoroughly.
3. Spoon into bowls. Serve with toppings of your choice.

Buckwheat Breakfast Bowl

Number of servings: 2

Nutritional values per serving:

Calories – 244, Fat – 3 g, Carbohydrate – 53 g, Fiber – NA, Protein – 7 g

Ingredients:

For bowl:

- ½ cup uncooked buckwheat, rinsed
- ½ teaspoon ground cinnamon
- 1 cup homemade almond milk
- 2 dates, pitted, finely chopped
- 1 cup water

For toppings:

- 1 tablespoon dried currants
- 1 tablespoon unsweetened shredded coconut
- ½ teaspoon ground cinnamon
- 1 tablespoon chopped walnuts

Directions:

1. Add buckwheat and water into a saucepan. Place saucepan over medium heat. Cook until soft. Turn off the heat.
2. Add milk into another saucepan. Place saucepan over medium-low heat. Add dates, buckwheat and cinnamon and stir.
3. Simmer until thick. Stir frequently once it begins to thicken.
4. Divide into 2 bowls.

5. Sprinkle toppings on top and serve.

Roasted Vegetable Bowls with Almond Butter Dressing

Number of servings: 2

Nutritional values per serving:

Calories – 450, Fat – 18.5 g, Carbohydrate – 45.7 g, Fiber – 14 g, Protein – 12.1 g

Ingredients:

For roasted vegetables:

- 2 small heads broccoli, cut into florets
- 1 clove garlic, minced
- Salt to taste
- Pepper to taste
- 1 large sweet potato, peeled, chopped into small cubes
- ½ tablespoon sesame oil or olive oil

For coconut mango rice:

- 1 teaspoon unrefined coconut oil
- ½ cup water
- 1 medium ripe mango, peeled, pitted, diced
- ½ cup coconut milk or almond coconut milk (from carton), unsweetened
- ½ cup uncooked brown rice, rinsed

For almond butter dressing:

- 2 tablespoons natural creamy almond butter
- 1 teaspoon pure maple syrup
- ½ teaspoon toasted sesame oil or melted coconut oil or olive oil
- 2 tablespoons fresh orange juice
- ¼ teaspoon apple cider vinegar

To garnish:

- 1 green onion, thinly sliced
- 2 teaspoons toasted sesame seeds
- A handful cilantro, chopped

Directions:

1. For coconut mango rice: Place a pot over medium- high heat. Add coconut oil. When the oil melts, add rice and stir-fry for 3-4 minutes until toasted lightly and turns opaque. Stir frequently.
2. Add water and coconut milk. When it begins to boil, lower the heat and cover with a lid.
3. Cook until dry. It should take about 30 minutes. Turn off the heat and let it sit covered for 10 minutes. Fluff the rice with a fork. Set aside for 10 minutes. Add mango and salt and stir lightly until mango pieces are evenly distributed in the rice.
4. Meanwhile, make the roasted vegetables as follow: Place a sheet of parchment paper on a baking sheet.
5. Place sweet potatoes in a microwave safe bowl. Microwave on High for 3 minutes.
6. Transfer on to the prepared baking sheet.
7. Place the broccoli florets on the baking sheet. Spread the sweet potatoes and broccoli in a single layer. Sprinkle garlic over it.
8. Roast in a preheated oven at 375° F for about 20-25 minutes or until tender. Turn the vegetables half way through roasting.
9. To make dressing: Add all the ingredients for dressing into a bowl and whisk well. Taste and adjust the seasonings if desired.
10. To arrange the bowls: Divide coconut mango rice into 2 bowls. Scatter the roasted vegetables over the rice.

11. Drizzle the dressing on top.
12. Garnish with cilantro, green onion and sesame seeds and serve.

Green Spring Vegetable Bowls & Creamy Chimichurri

Number of servings: 2

Nutritional values per serving:

Calories – 168, Fat – 8 g, Carbohydrate – 19 g, Fiber – 10 g, Protein – 9 g

Ingredients:

For veggie bowl:

- 1 small head cauliflower, cut into 2-3 slices
- ½ bunch asparagus, cut into bite size pieces
- 1 medium head cauliflower, cut into 2-3 slices
- 2 ½ cups fresh spinach leaves
- ¼ cup roasted sunflower seeds
- ½ cup pea shoots
- Salt to taste
- Pepper to taste

For creamy chimichurri:

- ½ avocado, peeled, pitted, chopped
- ½ cup fresh cilantro leaves (do not use stems)
- ¼ teaspoon dried oregano
- 2 small cloves garlic, peeled
- ¼ teaspoon salt or to taste
- 2-3 tablespoons water
- ¾ cup flat leaf parsley leaves (do not use stems)
- Juice of half lemon
- ¼ teaspoon red pepper flakes

Directions:

1. <u>For bowls:</u> Preheat a grill to medium heat. Grease the grill grates. Place cauliflower slices and broccoli slices on the grill and grill for 12-15 minutes.
2. Flip sides and grill the other side for 12-15 minutes. It should be well grilled but not burnt. You can also roast in an oven at 400° F for about 20-25 minutes or until tender. Turn the vegetables half way through roasting.
3. Meanwhile make chimichurri as follows: Add all the ingredients for chimichurri into a blender and blend until smooth. Transfer into a bowl. Cover and set aside for a while for the flavors to blend in.
4. Once roasted, remove from the grill/oven and place on a cutting board. When cool enough to handle, chop into pieces.
5. Add asparagus, spinach, cauliflower and broccoli into a bowl and toss well. Pour chimichurri over the vegetables and toss well.
6. Divide into 2 bowls.
7. Scatter pea shoots and sunflower seeds on top and serve.

Vanilla Quinoa and Roasted Blueberry Breakfast Bowl

Number of servings: 2

Nutritional values per serving: ½ cup

Calories – 226, Fat – 6 g, Carbohydrate – 36 g, Fiber – 5 g, Protein – 6 g

Ingredients:

- ½ cup quinoa
- ½ tablespoon vanilla
- ½ tablespoon coconut oil, melted
- Sea salt to taste
- 1 cup fresh or frozen blueberries + extra to serve
- 1 cup water
- ¼ teaspoon ground cinnamon
- ½ tablespoon vanilla extract

Directions:

1. Add blueberries, oil and cinnamon into a bowl and toss well. Transfer onto a baking sheet lined with parchment paper.
2. Roast in a preheated oven at 400° F for 12-15 minutes or until soft.
3. Add rest of the ingredients into a saucepan. Place the saucepan over medium heat.
4. When it begins to boil, lower the heat and cover with a lid. Simmer until dry. Turn off the heat. Let it sit covered for 5 minutes. Fluff with a fork
5. Divide quinoa into 2 bowls. Top with the roasted blueberries. Sprinkle some fresh blueberries on top and serve.

Chapter Five: Plant Based Breakfast Cereals (Oats, Quinoa, Chia seeds etc.)

Quinoa & Chia Oatmeal Mix

Number of servings: 6

Nutritional values per serving: 1/3-cup oatmeal mix, without serving options

Calories – 196, Fat – 4 g, Carbohydrate – 35 g, Fiber – 6 g, Protein – 6 g

Ingredients:

- 1 cup old-fashioned oats
- ½ cup quinoa
- ¼ cup chia seeds or hemp seeds
- 1/8 teaspoon salt
- ½ cup rolled wheat or barley flakes
- ½ cup dried fruit like raisins, chopped apricots or cranberries
- ½ teaspoon ground cinnamon

Serving day ingredients:

- 1 ¼ cups water or milk per serving
- Sweetener of your choice
- Nuts or dried fruit of your choice
- Any other toppings of your choice

Directions:

1. Add all the ingredients into an airtight container. Mix well. Cover and set aside at room temperature.
2. To serve: Add 1/3-cup quinoa into a saucepan. Pour water or milk and stir. Place the saucepan over medium heat.

3. When it begins to boil, lower the heat and cover partially with a lid. Cook until thick. Stir occasionally.
4. Turn off the heat and cover the saucepan fully. Let it sit for 5 minutes.
5. Add sweetener and mix well. Transfer into a bowl. Place the suggested toppings or any other toppings of your choice and serve.

Granola

Number of servings: 7

Nutritional values per serving: ¼ cup granola, without serving options

Calories – 93, Fat – 6 g, Carbohydrate – 9 g, Fiber – 1 g, Protein – 3 g

Ingredients:

- ¾ cup rolled oats
- ¼ cup sesame seeds or sunflower seeds
- 1 tablespoon melted coconut oil
- ¼ cup pumpkin seeds
- 1 tablespoon honey or agave nectar or maple syrup

Serving day ingredients:

- ½ cup Greek yogurt or soy yogurt or cashew yogurt per serving
- Toppings of your choice

Directions:

1. Add all the ingredients into a bowl and stir until well combined.
2. Transfer onto a baking sheet line with parchment paper. Spread it evenly.
3. Bake in a preheated oven at 350° F for about 15 minutes. Stir once, half way through baking.
4. Remove from the oven and cool completely. Transfer into an airtight container. Store at room temperature. . It can last for about 15 days.
5. To serve: Take ½ cup yogurt in a bowl. Add ¼ cup granola and toppings of your choice and serve.

Oat-Walnut Granola

Number of servings: 5

Nutritional values per serving: 1/3-cup granola with yogurt but no toppings

Calories – 269, Fat – 9 g, Carbohydrate – 35 g, Fiber – 4 g, Protein – 13 g

Ingredients:

- 1 cup regular rolled oats
- 6 tablespoons puffed kamut cereal or puffed wheat cereal
- ½ cup bran cereal flakes
- 3 tablespoons chopped walnuts
- 1 tablespoon canola oil
- A pinch salt
- 3 tablespoons sugar-free or light pancake syrup
- ¼ teaspoon ground cinnamon
- Cooking spray

Serving day ingredients:

- ½ cup yogurt per serving
- Toppings of your choice

Directions:

1. Grease a baking dish with cooking spray.
2. Add all the cereal and walnuts into a bowl and stir.
3. Add syrup, oil, salt and cinnamon into a bowl and stir. Pour over the cereal and toss until well combined.
4. Spread it evenly in the dish.
5. Bake in a preheated oven at 350° F for about 15 minutes. Stir once, half way through baking.

6. Remove from the oven and cool completely. Transfer into an airtight container. Store at room temperature. . It can last for about 15 days.
7. To serve: Take ½ cup yogurt in a bowl. Add 1/3-cup granola and toppings of your choice and serve.

Crunchy Granola Wedges

Number of servings: 4

Nutritional values per serving:

Calories – 279, Fat – 9 g, Carbohydrate – 47 g, Fiber – 5 g, Protein – 6 g

Ingredients:

- ½ cup rolled oats
- ½ cup sunflower seeds
- ½ cup wheat flakes
- 4 tablespoons honey or agave nectar or maple syrup
- A pinch salt
- ½ cup dried cranberries
- Cooking spray

Directions:

1. Place wheat flakes, oats and sunflower seeds on a baking sheet. Spread it evenly.
2. Bake in a preheated oven at 400° F until aromatic and light brown.
3. Grease a 6-inch pie pan with cooking spray.
4. Add honey into a small saucepan and heat until big bubbles appear. Turn off the heat.
5. Add the oat mixture, salt and cranberries immediately into the honey. Mix until well incorporated and the cereal mixture is well coated with the honey
6. Spoon into the pie pan. Grease a spatula with a little oil and smoothen the mixture in the pan.
7. Let it rest for 30 minutes. Cut into 4 wedges and place on a wire rack.
8. Cool completely.

Fall Oatmeal Power Bowl

Number of servings: 2

Nutritional values per serving:

Calories – 347, Fat – 13.9 g, Carbohydrate – NA g, Fiber – 16.6 g, Protein – 11.6 g

Ingredients:

- ½ cup steel cut oats
- 1 small banana (optional), sliced
- 2 teaspoons raw pumpkin seeds
- 2 teaspoons coconut sugar or maple syrup
- 1 teaspoon grated orange zest (optional), to garnish
- 2 cups almond milk
- ¼ teaspoon salt
- 1 medium apple, thinly sliced
- 1 teaspoon chia seeds
- ½ teaspoon ground cinnamon + extra to garnish

Directions:

1. Place a heavy bottom saucepan over high heat. Add almond milk and oats and stir.
2. Add salt and stir. When it begins to boil, lower the heat and cook until soft.
3. Add cinnamon and stir. Turn off the heat.
4. Divide into 2 bowls.
5. Add rest of the ingredients and stir. Garnish with orange zest and some cinnamon and serve.

Chocolate Peanut Butter Protein Baked Oatmeal Cups

Number of servings: 6

Nutritional values per serving: 1 muffin

Calories – 155, Fat – 5 g, Carbohydrate – 21 g, Fiber – 4 g, Protein – 6 g

Ingredients:

- 1 tablespoon chia seeds
- 3 tablespoons water
- ½ cup cashew milk or almond milk or coconut milk, unsweetened
- 2 tablespoons pure maple syrup or 7-8 drops liquid stevia
- 1 ½ cups old fashioned oats
- ½ scoop plant based chocolate protein powder
- 3 small to medium over-ripe bananas, mashed
- 2 tablespoons creamy peanut butter
- ¼ teaspoon vanilla extract
- 1 tablespoon cocoa powder
- A pinch salt
- ½ tablespoon baking powder

Directions:

1. Grease a 6 counts muffin tin with cooking spray.
2. To make chia eggs: Add chia seeds and water in a bowl. Stir and set aside to chill for a while. You can use 1 large egg instead, if you have no issues with including eggs in your diet.
3. Add bananas, milk, peanut butter, maple syrup or stevia and vanilla into a bowl and mix well.

4. Add chia seed mixture and mix well.
5. Add all the dry ingredients into another bowl and stir. Add into the bowl of wet ingredients and mix well.
6. Pour into the prepared pan. Fill up to ¾.
7. Bake in a preheated oven at 350° F for about 20-25 minutes or until a toothpick when inserted in the center comes out clean.
8. Cool on a wire rack. Remove from the molds and serve.
9. Left over ones can be stored in an airtight container in the refrigerator. It can last for 5-6 days in the refrigerator.

Roasted Banana Smash Oatmeal

Number of servings: 2

Nutritional values per serving:

Calories – 217, Fat – 3 g, Carbohydrate – 46 g, Fiber – 7 g, Protein – 5 g

Ingredients:

- ½ cup old fashioned oats
- 1 cup + 2 tablespoons unsweetened almond milk
- ½ teaspoon ground cinnamon
- 2 very ripe bananas, peeled

Directions:

1. Line a baking sheet with parchment paper. Place the bananas over it. Using a fork, smash the bananas with it.
2. Roast in a preheated oven at 400° F for about 12-15 minutes or until light golden brown.
3. Meanwhile, add oats, milk and cinnamon into a saucepan. Place the saucepan over medium heat.
4. When it begins to boil, lower the heat and simmer until oats are cooked and the mixture is thick as well.
5. Turn off the heat. Add roasted banana smash along with the cooked juices.
6. Mix well. Divide into bowls and serve.

Banana Apple Porridge

Number of servings: 2

Nutritional values per serving:

Calories – 70, Fat – 2 g, Carbohydrate – 35 g, Fiber – NA, Protein – 6 g

Ingredients:

- 8 tablespoons rolled oats
- 7 tablespoons bulgur, rinsed, drained
- ½ medium banana, chopped
- ½ medium apple, cored, chopped
- 2 cups low fat milk
- 2 tablespoons Earth balance butter
- 2 teaspoons powdered sugar
- 1 cup water

Directions:

1. Place a heavy bottomed pan over medium heat. Add Earth balance. When it melts, add bulgur and sauté for a few minutes until light brown and aromatic.
2. Add oats and stir. Cook until aromatic.
3. Stir in milk and water. When it begins to boil, lower the heat and cover with a lid.
4. Simmer until bulgur is tender. It can take about 30 minutes to cook. You can make it in a pressure cooker if you own one. It is much quicker.
5. Stir in powdered sugar and cinnamon.
6. Ladle into bowls. Divide the banana and apple slice equally among the bowls and serve.

Coconut Overnight Oatmeal

Number of servings: 2

Nutritional values per serving:

Calories – 287, Fat – 8 g, Carbohydrate – 51 g, Fiber – NA, Protein – 6 g

Ingredients:

- 2/3 cup old-fashioned rolled oats
- ¼ teaspoon salt
- 2 tablespoons hazelnuts
- 2/3 cup coconut milk, unsweetened
- 2/3 cup dried, chopped apricots
- 2 teaspoons maple syrup

Directions:

1. Add coconut milk, oats and salt into a bowl and stir. Cover and chill for 8-9 hours.
2. Stir and divide into 2 bowls.
3. Garnish with hazelnuts and apricots.
4. Drizzle maple syrup on top and serve.

Flat-Belly Overnight Oats

Number of servings: 2

Nutritional values per serving:

Calories – 336, Fat – 9.3 g, Carbohydrate – 55.9 g, Fiber – 9.5 g, Protein – 10.8 g

Ingredients:

- 1 cup rolled oats
- ½ teaspoon ground cinnamon
- ½ cup yogurt or soy yogurt
- ½ cup chopped pineapple
- 2 tablespoons chopped almonds
- 2 teaspoons chia seeds
- 1 cup unsweetened vanilla almond milk
- ½ banana, sliced
- ½ cup blueberries, fresh or frozen

Directions:

1. Divide the oats among 2 mason's jars. Divide half the chia seeds and sprinkle over the oats. Sprinkle cinnamon in each jar.
2. Pour half the milk in each jar followed by half the yogurt.
3. Layer with half of each - banana slices, pineapple, blueberries and almonds in each jar. Fasten the lid of the jars.
4. Chill overnight.
5. Stir and serve cold or heat in a microwave and serve.

Creamy Polenta

Number of servings: 4

Nutritional values per serving:

Calories – 74, Fat – 1 g, Carbohydrate – 16 g, Fiber – 1 g, Protein – 2 g

Ingredients:

- 14 tablespoons cornmeal
- ½ teaspoon salt
- 3 cups cold water

Directions:

1. Add cornmeal, salt and water into a saucepan. Place the saucepan over medium heat.
2. Stir constantly until slightly thick.
3. Cover the pan with a lid, partially.
4. Lower the heat and simmer for 15-20 minutes or until very thick. Stir frequently.
5. Turn off the heat. Cover it completely. Let it rest for 10 minutes.
6. Stir and divide into 4 bowls.
7. Serve hot or warm.

Pumpkin Pie Breakfast Sorghum

Number of servings: 2

Nutritional values per serving:

Calories – 221, Fat – 3g, Carbohydrate – 47 g, Fiber – 5 g, Protein – 10 g

Ingredients:

- 6 tablespoons pumpkin puree
- ½ cup sorghum, rinsed
- ½ tablespoon pumpkin pie spice
- ½ cup almond milk, unsweetened + extra to serve
- 1 tablespoon pure maple syrup
- ½ teaspoon pure vanilla extract
- 1 cup water

Directions:

1. Add all the ingredients into a heavy bottomed pan. Mix well.
2. Place the pan over medium heat. When the mixture begins to boil, lower the heat and cover with a lid. Stir frequently and cook until soft.
3. Divide into 2 bowls. Serve with a little almond milk.

Dark Chocolate Pumpkin Oatmeal

Number of servings: 4

Nutritional values per serving:

Calories – 234, Fat – 7 g, Carbohydrate – 41 g, Fiber – 5 g, Protein – 5 g

Ingredients:

- 2 cups almond milk
- 1 teaspoon ground cinnamon
- ½ teaspoon ground cloves
- ½ teaspoon ground nutmeg
- 1 cup rolled oats
- 2 tablespoons dark chocolate, unsweetened
- 4 tablespoons honey or agave nectar or maple syrup
- 2 tablespoons slivered almonds
- 1 cup plain pumpkin puree
- 2 tablespoons dried cherries

Directions:

1. Place a saucepan over medium heat. Add almond milk.
2. When it begins to boil, lower heat. Add oats and simmer until the oats are cooked.
3. Add cinnamon, cloves, nutmeg and chocolate and cook until the chocolate melts. Stir frequently.
4. Add honey and pumpkin and mix well. Heat thoroughly and remove from heat.
5. Serve in bowls. Garnish with almonds and cherries and serve.

Three-Grain Porridge

Number of servings: 9

Nutritional values per serving: 1.8 ounces porridge mix without serving options

Calories – 179, Fat – 2 g, Carbohydrate – 32 g, Fiber – 4 g, Protein – 7 g

Ingredients:

- 5.3 ounces oatmeal
- 5.3 ounces barley flakes
- 5.3 ounces spelt flakes

Serving day ingredients:

- Sliced strawberries
- Agave nectar
- 1 ½ cups milk or water per serving

Directions:

1. Place a pan over medium heat. Add oatmeal and lightly toast it. Spread into a bowl and cool completely.
2. Similarly toast the spelt flakes and barley flakes and cool completely.
3. Transfer into an airtight container and mix well. Fasten the lid and store at room temperature.
4. To serve: Add milk or water and 1.8 ounces porridge mix (for 1 serving). Place the saucepan over medium heat. Cook until thick.
5. Pour into a bowl. Top with strawberries. Drizzle agave nectar on top and serve.

Savory Curry Cashew Oatmeal

Number of servings: 2

Nutritional values per serving: 1-¼ cups

Calories – 332, Fat –11 g, Carbohydrate – 55 g, Fiber – 6 g, Protein – 9 g

Ingredients:

- 1 cup old fashioned rolled oats
- 2 cups water
- Salt to taste
- ½ teaspoon curry powder
- ¼ cup cashews, chopped, toasted
- 1/3 cup golden raisins

Directions:

1. Pour water into a saucepan. Add salt. When the water begins to boil, add oats and mix well.
2. Lower the heat to low heat and cook until nearly dry.
3. Remove from heat. Cover the saucepan and let it sit for 2-3 minutes.
4. Add curry powder, cashews and raisins and mix well.
5. Spoon into bowls and serve.

Breakfast Oatmeal Risotto

Number of servings: 2

Nutritional values per serving:

Calories – 223, Fat – 10 g, Carbohydrate – 31 g, Fiber – NA, Protein – 9 g

Ingredients:

- 1 tablespoon olive oil
- 1 clove garlic, minced
- 2 tablespoons minced green bell pepper
- ¼ small onion, minced
- ½ cup minced mushrooms
- ½ cup steel cut oats
- 2 – 2 ½ cups water or more if required
- 1 tablespoon minced sun dried tomatoes
- ¼ teaspoon dried marjoram
- ½ teaspoon dried oregano
- ½ teaspoon dried basil
- A pinch dried rosemary
- 1 tablespoons nutritional yeast
- Salt to taste
- Pepper to taste

Directions:

1. Place a Dutch oven or heavy bottomed pan over medium heat. Add oil. When oil is heated, add onions and sauté until slightly pink.
2. Stir in the garlic, mushrooms, bell pepper and dried herbs.
3. Sauté until the mushrooms are brown. Add oats and stir constantly until it is lightly toasted.

4. Add sundried tomatoes and about 1 cup of water. When it begins to boil, lower the heat and cover with a lid.
5. Stir often.
6. Add another cup of water and continue simmering, stirring often.
7. Continue adding water, a little at a time, until the oats are tender. Add more water if required.
8. Add nutritional yeast, salt and pepper. Mix well and serve immediately.

Crispy Quinoa Cakes

Number of servings: 24

Nutritional values per serving: 1 cake

Calories – 90, Fat – 3.5 g, Carbohydrate – 13 g, Fiber – 2 g, Protein – 3 g

Ingredients:

- 3 cups cooked quinoa
- 2 cups chopped kale (discard hard stems and ribs)
- 1 cup grated sweet potato
- 1 cup rolled oats, finely ground
- 4 tablespoons ground flaxseeds
- 12 tablespoons water
- ¼ cup chopped onions
- ½ cup finely chopped fresh basil leaves
- ½ cup sunflower seeds
- ½ cup chopped, oil packed sun dried tomatoes
- 2 cloves garlic, minced
- 2 tablespoons watery tahini paste
- 3 teaspoons red or white wine vinegar
- 3 teaspoons dried oregano
- 1 teaspoon fine grain sea salt or to taste
- 6 tablespoons gluten-free all-purpose flour or regular all-purpose flour
- 1 teaspoon red pepper flakes or to taste

Directions:

1. Mix together flaxseeds and water in a mixing bowl. Place in the refrigerator for 15 minutes. This is flax egg.
2. Mix together all the ingredients in a large bowl. Add flaxseed mixture and water and mix well.

3. Divide the mixture into 24 equal portions and shape into patties. Place the patties on a large lined baking sheet in a single layer. Bake in batches if necessary.
4. Bake in a preheated oven at 400°F for about 15 minutes. Flip sides and bake for 10 minutes or until golden brown.
5. Serve hot.

Vegetables & Creamy Polenta Recipe

Number of servings: 2

Nutritional values per serving:

Calories – 360, Fat – 6 g, Carbohydrate – 57 g, Fiber – 10 g, Protein – 21 g

Ingredients:

- ½ cup cornmeal
- 7 ounces vegetable broth
- 1 ½ cups chopped red bell peppers
- 1 ½ cups chopped zucchini
- 1 can (14 ounces) diced tomatoes, with its liquid
- 1 cup fat-free milk
- ¼ cup grated parmesan cheese, divided
- ½ onion, chopped
- ½ envelope (from a 0.7 ounce packet) Italian dressing mix

Directions:

1. Add cornmeal, broth, milk and 2 tablespoons cheese into a microwave safe bowl. Whisk well.
2. Microwave on high for about 15 minutes or until thick. Stir every 4-5 minutes.
3. In the meantime, add vegetables and dressing mix into a pan. Place the pan over medium heat and cook until the vegetables are crisp as well as tender. Stir often.
4. Divide polenta into 2 bowls.
5. Top with vegetable mixture. Sprinkle remaining cheese on top and serve.

Chapter Six: Plant Based Breakfast Wrap, Burrito and Taco Recipes

Edamame Hummus Wrap

Number of servings: 2

Nutritional values per serving: 1 wrap

Calories – 339, Fat – 20 g, Carbohydrate – 35 g, Fiber – 8 g, Protein – 14 g

Ingredients:

- 6 ounces frozen shelled edamame, thawed
- 1 ½ tablespoons extra-virgin olive oil, divided
- 1 small clove garlic, chopped
- Pepper to taste
- 1 cup very thinly sliced green cabbage
- 1 small scallion, thinly sliced
- 2 spinach or whole wheat tortillas (8 inches each)

- 2 tablespoons lemon juice, divided
- 1 tablespoon tahini
- ¼ teaspoon ground cumin
- ¼ teaspoon salt or to taste
- ¼ cup sliced orange bell pepper
- A handful fresh parsley, chopped

Directions:

1. To make edamame hummus: Add edamame, 1 tablespoon oil, 1 ½ tablespoons lemon juice, salt, pepper, cumin, garlic and tahini into the food processor bowl and process until smooth.
2. Pour into a bowl.
3. Add pepper, remaining oil and lemon juice into another bowl and whisk well. Stir in the bell pepper, cabbage, parsley and scallion. Mix until well coated.
4. Place tortillas on your countertop. Smear about ½ cup of edamame hummus over it on 1/3 of the lower portion of the tortilla.
5. Spread ½ cup of the cabbage mixture.
6. Roll and serve.

Greek Salad Wraps

Number of servings:

Nutritional values per serving: 1 wrap filled with 1 ½ cups salad

Calories – 333, Fat – 14 g, Carbohydrate – 42 g, Fiber – 7 g, Protein – 9 g

Ingredients:

For dressing:

- 3 tablespoons red wine vinegar
- 1 tablespoon fresh oregano, minced
- 2 tablespoons extra-virgin olive oil
- Salt to taste
- Pepper to taste

For wrap:

- 4 cups chopped romaine lettuce
- 1 small cucumber, halved, sliced
- 2 tablespoons pitted, sliced kalamata olives
- 3 whole wheat wraps (8-9 inches each)
- ½ can (from a 15 ounces can) chickpeas, drained
- ½ cup halved cherry tomatoes or grape tomatoes
- 1 small onion, thinly sliced

Directions:

1. To make dressing: Add all the ingredients for dressing into a bowl and whisk well. Add lettuce, cucumber, olives, chickpeas, tomatoes and onion and mix well.
2. Place the wraps on your countertop. Divide the salad among the wraps. Roll and serve.

Red Pepper, Goat Cheese, and Fresh Mint Wraps

Number of servings: 2

Nutritional values per serving: 1 wrap

Calories – 254, Fat – 9 g, Carbohydrate – 33 g, Fiber – 2 g, Protein – 10 g

Ingredients:

- 2 ounces goat's cheese
- 2 spinach tortillas (8 inches each)
- Salt to taste
- 2 tablespoons chopped fresh mint
- ¼ cup chopped, roasted red bell peppers

Directions:

1. Add cheese and mint leaves into a bowl and stir.
2. Warm the tortillas following the instructions on the package.
3. Place tortillas on 2 serving plates. Divide the cheese mixture among the tortillas.
4. Scatter 2 tablespoons roasted red peppers on each.
5. Roll the tortillas and cover the wraps with cling wrap. Refrigerate for an hour.
6. Slice and serve.

Salsa Tofu Breakfast Burrito

Number of servings: 2

Nutritional values per serving:

Calories – 259, Fat – 13 g, Carbohydrate – 30 g, Fiber – 4 g, Protein – 15 g

Ingredients:

- 2 teaspoons extra-virgin olive oil
- ½ cup fresh salsa
- Freshly ground pepper to taste
- 2 whole wheat tortillas (8 inches each)
- 1 cup extra firm tofu, crumbled
- Salt to taste
- ½ cup grated Monterey Jack cheese or vegan cheese

Directions:

1. Place a nonstick skillet over medium heat. Add oil. When the oil is heated, add tofu. Sauté until light brown.
2. Add salsa, salt and pepper. Mix well and heat thoroughly.
3. Place tortillas on a serving platter. Scatter cheese along the diameter of the tortillas.
4. Divide the tofu mixture and place over the cheese.
5. Wrap into a burrito and serve.

Mexican Breakfast Burritos

Number of servings: 3

Nutritional values per serving:

Calories – 329, Fat – 10 g, Carbohydrate – 45 g, Fiber – 8 g, Protein – 15 g

Ingredients:

- 1 tablespoon avocado oil, divided
- 1 teaspoon chili powder
- ½ teaspoon salt or to taste
- 2 cups frozen corn, thawed
- 1 cup fresh salsa
- 3 whole wheat tortillas or wraps (8 inches each)
- ½ package (from a 14 ounces package) extra-firm water-packed tofu, drained, crumbled
- ½ teaspoon ground cumin
- ½ can (from a 15 ounces can) black beans, rinsed, drained
- 2 scallions, sliced
- A handful fresh cilantro, chopped

Directions:

1. Place a nonstick skillet over medium flame. Add half the oil. When the oil is heated, add tofu, salt and spices and cook until brown.
2. Remove the tofu into a bowl.
3. Place the skillet back over heat with remaining oil. When oil is heated, stir in the beans, scallions and corn and cook until scallions are soft.
4. Add the tofu back into the skillet. Stir in salsa and cilantro and heat thoroughly.
5. Place tortillas on a serving platter.

6. Divide the tofu mixture among the tortillas and place over it on 1/3 of the lower portion of the tortillas.
7. Wrap into a burrito and serve.

Chipotle Bean Burritos

Number of servings: 3

Nutritional values per serving: 1 burrito

Calories – 361, Fat – 10.3 g, Carbohydrate – 52.2 g, Fiber – 11.4 g, Protein – 16.8 g

Ingredients:

- 1 ½ teaspoons canola oil
- ¼ teaspoon chipotle chili powder
- 1-2 tablespoons water
- ½ can (from a 15 ounces can) kidney beans, drained
- ½ can from (a 15 ounces can) black beans, drained
- 2 whole wheat tortillas (10 inches each)
- ¾ cup chopped plum tomatoes
- 3 tablespoons chopped green onion
- ½ cup thin lettuce strips
- 1 ½ tablespoons fresh salsa, chilled
- Salt or to taste
- 2 small cloves garlic, minced
- ½ cup reduced fat, shredded 4 - cheese Mexican blend
- 3 tablespoons light sour cream

Directions:

1. Place a nonstick skillet over medium heat. Add oil. When oil is heated, add garlic and sauté until light brown.
2. Add chili powder and salt and stir constantly for a few seconds. Add water and beans.
3. When it begins to boil, lower the heat to low heat and cover with a lid. Simmer for about 10 minutes. Turn off the heat and add salsa. Mix well and slightly mash the beans with the back of a spoon.

4. Warm the tortillas following the instructions on the package. Divide the bean mixture into 3 equal portions and place in the center of each tortilla, along the diameter.
5. Divide the cheese, tomatoes, lettuce, green onion and sour cream and place over the bean mixture. Wrap like a burrito and serve.

Roasted Chickpea and Broccoli Burrito

Number of servings: 4

Nutritional values per serving:

Calories – 301, Fat – 9 g, Carbohydrate – 45 g, Fiber – 10 g, Protein – 10 g

Ingredients:

- 1 can (15 ounces) unsalted chickpeas, rinsed, drained
- ½ red bell pepper, chopped
- 1 ½ tablespoons olive oil
- 1 medium yellow onion, chopped
- 2 cloves garlic, minced
- ½ pound broccoli, chopped
- 1 tablespoon low- sodium soy sauce
- ½ teaspoon ground cumin
- ¼ teaspoon ground coriander
- 1 teaspoon chili powder
- ½ teaspoon smoked paprika
- Cayenne pepper to taste
- 4 tortillas (8 inches each)
- Juice of a lime

Directions:

1. Add chickpeas, broccoli, onion and pepper into a bowl and toss well.
2. Transfer on to a rimmed baking sheet. Bake in a preheated oven at 425° F for 20 minutes.
3. Place garlic on the baking sheet and continue baking for 15 minutes. Remove from the oven. Transfer into a bowl.
4. Add lemon juice and mix well.

5. Follow the instructions on the package and warm the tortillas. Divide and place the chickpea mixture over the tortillas. Wrap like a burrito and serve.

Breakfast Tacos

Number of servings: 3

Nutritional values per serving:

Calories – 245, Fat – 9.3g, Carbohydrate – 31.6 g, Fiber – 7.1 g, Protein – 12.3 g

Ingredients:

For "Bacon" Chickpeas:

- ½ can (from a 15 ounces can) chickpeas, drained
- ½ tablespoon tamari or soy sauce
- ½ teaspoon maple syrup
- Salt to taste
- Pepper to taste
- ½ tablespoon olive oil
- 1 teaspoon sriracha sauce
- ¼ teaspoon smoked paprika

For roasted tomatoes:

- ½ cup halved cherry tomatoes
- 2 small clove garlic, minced
- ½ tablespoon olive oil

For scrambled tofu:

- 6 ounces firm silken tofu
- 1 tablespoon hummus
- Salt to taste
- Pepper to taste
- 2 tablespoon nutritional yeast
- 1/8 teaspoon ground turmeric

To serve:

- 3 corn tortillas or flour tortillas
- Avocado slices
- Lime juice
- A handful fresh parsley, chopped
- Dairy-free yogurt to drizzle
- 1 radish, sliced

Directions:

1. For making "bacon" chickpeas: Dry the chickpeas by patting with paper towels. Add into a bowl along with rest of the ingredients for bacon chickpeas. Toss well.
2. Line a large baking sheet with parchment paper. Spread chickpea mixture on one half of the baking sheet.
3. To make roasted tomatoes: Add all the ingredients for roasted tomatoes into a bowl and toss well. Spread the tomatoes on the other half of the baking sheet.
4. Bake in a preheated oven at 400°F for about 20 minutes or until chickpeas are crisp and the tomatoes are slightly charred.
5. To make scrambled tofu: Place a nonstick skillet over medium heat. Add all the ingredients for tofu scramble into a skillet. Cook until slightly brown.
6. Turn off the heat.
7. To assemble: Place tortillas on serving plates. Divide the tofu scramble among the tortillas. Scatter chickpeas and tomatoes over the scramble.
8. Place toppings and serve.

Healthy Breakfast Tacos with Tofu & Roasted Potatoes

Number of servings: 3

Nutritional values per serving: Without optional toppings

Calories – 196, Fat – 4 g, Carbohydrate – 34 g, Fiber – 5 g, Protein – 9 g

Ingredients:

For roasted potatoes:

- ¾ pound red potatoes, scrubbed, pat dried, cubed
- 1 bell pepper of any color, chopped into ½ inch squares
- 1 small yellow onion, chopped into ½ inch pieces
- ½ teaspoon lemon juice
- ½ teaspoon smoked paprika
- ½ jalapeño, sliced
- ½ teaspoon salt or to taste
- ¼ teaspoon garlic powder

For scrambled tofu:

- 6 ounces firm silken tofu
- 1 tablespoon hummus
- Salt to taste
- Pepper to taste
- 2 tablespoon nutritional yeast
- 1/8 teaspoon ground turmeric

To serve:

- 3 corn tortillas or flour tortillas

Optional toppings

- Avocado slices
- Lime juice
- A handful fresh parsley, chopped
- Salsa to drizzle
- Chao cheese slices
- Etc.

Directions:

1. Line a large baking sheet with parchment paper.
2. To make roasted potatoes: Add all the ingredients for roasted potatoes into a bowl and toss well. Spread the tomatoes on the other half of the baking sheet.
3. Bake in a preheated oven at 400° F for about 20-30 minutes or until the potatoes are cooked. Stir every 10-12 minutes.
4. To make scrambled tofu: Place a nonstick skillet over medium heat. Add all the ingredients for tofu scramble into a skillet. Cook until slightly brown.
5. Turn off the heat.
6. To assemble: Place tortillas on serving plates. Divide the tofu scramble among the tortillas. Divide the potato mixture and place over the tofu.
7. Place optional toppings on top and serve.

Black Bean and Tofu Breakfast Tostadas

Number of servings: 2

Nutritional values per serving: Without toppings

Calories – 380, Fat – 19 g, Carbohydrate – 35 g, Fiber – 11 g, Protein – 24 g

Ingredients:

For spicy black beans:

- 1 teaspoon olive oil
- 2 tablespoons chopped onion
- ½ can (from a 15 ounces can) black beans, drained, rinsed
- 1 tablespoon salsa
- 1 clove garlic, minced
- Salt to taste
- ½ teaspoon ground cumin
- ½ teaspoon chili powder
- ½ teaspoon dried oregano

For tofu scramble:

- 7 ounces firm tofu, pressed of excess moisture
- ¼ teaspoon turmeric powder
- ½ tablespoon olive oil
- 1 ½ tablespoons nutritional yeast
- Salt to taste

For crispy baked tortillas:

- ½ tablespoon olive oil
- 2 corn tortillas

Directions:

1. Place a skillet over medium flame. Add 1-teaspoon oil. When the oil is heated, add garlic and sauté until aromatic.
2. Stir in the onions and salt and cook until translucent.
3. Stir in the beans and all the spices and heat thoroughly. Turn off the heat and add into a bowl.
4. Mash the beans lightly with a fork. Add salsa and stir.
5. To make scramble: Place a nonstick skillet over medium heat. Add oil. When the oil is heated, add tofu, turmeric powder, salt and nutritional yeast and mix well. Heat thoroughly. Turn off the heat.
6. Place tortillas on a baking tray. Brush both sides of the tortillas with oil.
7. Bake in a preheated oven at 400° F for about 10 minutes or until crisp. Flip sides half way through baking.
8. To serve: Divide the mashed beans equally and spread over the tortillas.
9. Divide the tofu among the tortillas. Place toppings of choice and serve.

Chapter Seven: Plant Based Breakfast Pudding and Parfait Recipes

Blackberry and Chia Breakfast Pudding

Number of servings: 2

Nutritional values per serving: ½ cup

Calories – 211, Fat – 12 g, Carbohydrate – 19 g, Fiber – 5 g, Protein – 8 g

Ingredients:

- ¼ cup fresh blackberries
- ½ cup coconut milk, unsweetened
- 1/8 teaspoon almond extract
- ½ tablespoon unsweetened shredded coconut
- 1 ½ tablespoons chia seeds
- ¼ cup plain Greek yogurt
- 1 tablespoon honey or agave nectar or maple syrup
- 2 tablespoons toasted, sliced almonds, to garnish

Directions:

1. Place blackberries in a bowl. Mash with a fork.
2. Add rest of the ingredients and mix well. Cover and chill overnight.
3. Stir and divide into 2 bowls. Sprinkle a tablespoon of almonds on top of each bowl and serve.

Gingerbread Chia Pudding

Number of servings: 2

Nutritional values per serving:

Calories – 307, Fat – 17.8 g, Carbohydrate – 36.8 g, Fiber – 12.8 g, Protein – 13.5 g

Ingredients:

For pudding:

- ½ cup chia seeds
- 2 tablespoons maple syrup
- ½ teaspoon ground cinnamon
- A large pinch sea salt
- 1 ½ cups nondairy milk of your choice
- ½ teaspoon ground ginger
- ¼ teaspoon ground cloves

For toppings:

- 2 tablespoons chopped pecans or any nuts of your choice
- 2 tablespoons raisins

Directions:

1. Add all the ingredients for pudding into a bowl and stir until well incorporated.
2. Cover and chill overnight. Stir a couple of times if possible after a couple of hours of chilling.
3. Stir and spoon into bowls. Sprinkle raisins and nuts on top and serve.

Chocolate Chia Pudding with Raspberries

Number of servings: 2

Nutritional values per serving: 1 cup

Calories – 222, Fat – 11 g, Carbohydrate – 28 g, Fiber – 13 g, Protein – 6 g

Ingredients:

- 1 cup almond milk, unsweetened or any other milk of your choice
- 4 teaspoons maple syrup
- ½ teaspoon vanilla extract
- 2 tablespoons toasted, slivered almonds, divided
- 4 tablespoons chia seeds
- 1 teaspoon cocoa powder, unsweetened
- 1 cup fresh raspberries, divided

Directions:

1. Add milk, maple syrup, vanilla, chia seeds and cocoa into a bowl. Whisk well.
2. Cover and chill overnight.
3. Stir well. Take 2 glasses and place ½ cup of chia pudding in each glass.
4. Scatter ¼ cup raspberries in each glass. Sprinkle ½ tablespoon almonds in each glass.
5. Layer with ¼ cup chia pudding followed by ¼ cup raspberries in each glass.
6. Sprinkle ½ tablespoon almonds in each glass and serve.

Mango Coconut Chia Pudding

Number of servings: 2

Nutritional values per serving: 1 cup

Calories – 229, Fat – 11 g, Carbohydrate – 32 g, Fiber – 10 g, Protein – 5 g

Ingredients:

- 1 cup coconut milk, unsweetened or any other milk of your choice
- 4 teaspoons maple syrup
- 1 cup diced fresh mango, divided
- 4 tablespoons chia seeds
- ½ teaspoon coconut extract
- 2 tablespoons toasted unsweetened coconut chips, divided

Directions:

1. Add milk, maple syrup, coconut extract and chia seeds into a bowl. Whisk well.
2. Cover and chill overnight.
3. Stir well. Take 2 glasses and place ½ cup of chia pudding in each glass.
4. Scatter ¼ cup mangoes in each glass. Sprinkle ½ tablespoon coconut chips in each glass.
5. Layer with ¼ cup chia pudding followed by ¼ cup mangoes in each glass.
6. Sprinkle ½ tablespoon coconut chips in each glass and serve.

Orange Chia Pudding

Number of servings: 4

Nutritional values per serving: Without toppings

Calories – 127, Fat – 6 g, Carbohydrate – 14 g, Fiber – 7 g, Protein – 4 g

Ingredients:

- 6 blood oranges, peeled, separated into segments, deseeded
- 1 teaspoon ground cinnamon
- 1 ½ cups light coconut milk
- 2/3 cup chia seeds

Directions:

1. Add oranges, cinnamon and coconut milk into a blender and blend until smooth.
2. Pour into a bowl. Add chia seeds and stir.
3. Cover and chill for 7-8 hours.
4. Divide into bowls. Serve with toppings of your choice if desired.

Strawberry, Almond Butter and Oatmeal Breakfast Parfait

Number of servings: 4

Nutritional values per serving:

Calories – 332, Fat – 13 g, Carbohydrate – 49 g, Fiber – 12 g, Protein – 7 g

Ingredients:

- 1 cup rolled oats
- ½ cup almond milk
- 2 tablespoons almond butter
- 2 cups sliced fresh strawberry + extra to garnish
- 4 bananas, sliced, frozen
- 2 cups water
- 2 teaspoons vanilla
- 2 tablespoons almonds, sliced to garnish

Directions:

1. Place a saucepan over low heat. Add oats and water and cook for 7-8 minutes.
2. Add almond milk, almond butter and vanilla and stir until the mixture is well incorporated.
3. Remove from heat and cool until warm.
4. Add bananas and strawberries into a blender and blend until smooth.
5. To assemble: Take 4 parfait glasses. Divide the oats mixture into the glasses. Divide equally and pour the blended strawberries over the oat layer.
6. Sprinkle almonds over it. Place slices of strawberries on top and serve.

Peach Pie Breakfast Parfait

Number of servings: 2

Nutritional values per serving:

Calories – 260, Fat – 13 g, Carbohydrate – 30 g, Fiber – 8 g, Protein – 6 g

Ingredients:

- 2 tablespoons chia seeds
- ½ cup coconut milk
- 3 small peaches, pitted, diced
- 2 tablespoons pure maple syrup
- 2 teaspoons ground cinnamon
- 1 1/3 cup granola

Directions:

1. Add chia seeds, milk and maple syrup into a bowl. Stir and cover with a lid. Chill for a couple of hours.
2. Meanwhile, place the peaches in a bowl. Sprinkle cinnamon over it. Toss well and set aside.
3. Take 2 parfait glasses. Divide equally the chia pudding among the glasses.
4. Sprinkle ½ cup granola in each glass.
5. Divide the peaches among the glasses.
6. Sprinkle remaining granola on top and serve.

Chapter Eight: Plant Based Breakfast Pancake, Waffle, Crepe and Omelet Recipes

Vegan Pancakes

Number of servings: 3

Nutritional values per serving: 2 pancakes (4 inches each) without toppings

Calories – 174, Fat – 6 g, Carbohydrate – 27 g, Fiber – 3 g, Protein – 6 g

Ingredients:

For pancake:

- ¾ cup white whole wheat flour
- 1/8 teaspoon salt
- 2 tablespoons applesauce, unsweetened
- ½ tablespoon organic sugar or 1 tablespoon maple syrup
- 1 teaspoon baking powder

- ¾ cup almond milk or non-dairy milk of your choice, unsweetened
- ½ teaspoon vanilla extract
- 1 tablespoon coconut oil
- Cooking spray

To serve: Use any, as required (optional)

- Fruits of your choice
- Maple syrup
- Seeds or nuts
- Any other toppings of your choice

Directions:

1. Add all the dry ingredients for pancake into a bowl and stir. Add all the wet ingredients for pancake into another bowl and whisk until well combined.
2. Pour the wet ingredients into the bowl of dry ingredients and whisk until just combined. Do not whisk for long. Cover and set aside for 15 minutes.
3. Place a nonstick skillet over medium heat. Spray with cooking spray. Pour 3-4 tablespoons of batter in the center of the pan. Swirl the pan slightly so that the batter spreads (about 4 inches diameter). In a while, bubbles will begin to appear on the pancake. Cook until the underside is golden brown.
4. Flip sides and cook the other side as well. Remove onto a plate and keep warm.
5. Repeat steps 2-3 and make pancakes with the remaining batter.
6. Serve with suggested toppings if desired.

Gingerbread Pancakes

Number of servings: 2

Nutritional values per serving: 4 small pancakes

Calories – 77, Fat – 1.9 g, Carbohydrate – 10.6 g, Fiber – 0.7 g, Protein – 4 g

Ingredients:

For flax egg:

- ½ tablespoon ground flaxseed mixed with 1 ½ tablespoons water

For dry ingredients:

- ½ cup whole wheat flour
- ¼ teaspoon baking soda
- ½ teaspoon baking powder
- ½ scoop plant based vanilla protein powder
- ¼ teaspoon ground ginger
- ½ teaspoon ground cinnamon
- A pinch ground cloves
- 1/8 teaspoon freshly grated nutmeg

For wet ingredients:

- ½ teaspoon apple cider vinegar
- 2 tablespoons canola oil
- ¾ cup vanilla soy milk
- 2 tablespoons pure maple syrup
- 1 teaspoon vanilla extract
- Cooking spray

Directions:

1. To make flax egg: Mix together flaxseeds and water in a small bowl and keep in the refrigerator for 15 minutes.
2. Meanwhile, mix together all the dry ingredients in a bowl.
3. To make vegan buttermilk: Mix together in another bowl, apple cider vinegar and soymilk. Add rest of the wet ingredients. Mix well. Add flax egg and mix well.
4. Add this mixture to the bowl of dry ingredients. Whisk until the entire contents are just combined. Do not over mix.
5. Place a nonstick pan over medium heat. When the pan is heated, spray the pan with cooking spray. Pour 2 tablespoons of batter on the pan. Spread into a small round pancake of about 4 inches by swirling the pan. Slowly bubbles will start forming. Cook until the underside is medium brown in color. Flip sides and cook the other side as well.
6. If your pan is big enough, then make the pancakes in batches.
7. Repeat steps 5 and 6 and make pancakes with the remaining batter.
8. Keep warm in the oven until use.

Chocolate Chip Banana Pancakes

Number of servings: 3

Nutritional values per serving: 1 pancake without serving options

Calories – 271, Fat – 16 g, Carbohydrate – 32 g, Fiber – 4 g, Protein – 5 g

Ingredients:

- 1 medium overripe banana, mashed
- 1 ½ tablespoons coconut oil, melted
- ¾ cup whole wheat flour
- ¼ cup vegan chocolate chips
- 1 tablespoon coconut sugar
- ½ cup coconut milk
- ½ teaspoon baking soda

Serving options:

- Maple syrup
- Berries
- Coconut butter
- Fruit of your choice
- Etc.

Directions:

1. Whisk together banana, sugar, milk and oil in a bowl.
2. Add flour and baking soda and whisk until just incorporated. Do not over-whisk.
3. Add chocolate chips and fold gently.
4. Place a nonstick pan over medium heat. When the pan is heated, spray the pan with cooking spray. Pour about 4 tablespoons of batter on the pan. Swirl the pan to

spread the pancake. Slowly bubbles will start forming. Cook until the underside is medium brown in color. Flip sides and cook the other side as well.
5. Remove the pancake and keep warm.
6. Repeat step 4-5 and make the remaining pancakes.

Crunchy Dill Chickpea Pancakes with Lemon-Garlic Aioli

Number of servings: 14

Nutritional values per serving: 1 pancake of 3 inches each with a teaspoon mayonnaise

Calories – 90, Fat – 6 g, Carbohydrate – 6 g, Fiber – 1 g, Protein – 2 g

Ingredients:

For lemon garlic aioli:

- ¼ cup vegan mayonnaise
- 1 teaspoon fresh lemon juice or more to taste
- 1 small clove garlic, grated

For pancakes:

- ½ tablespoon coconut oil or extra-virgin olive oil
- ¼ cup grated carrot
- ¼ cup chickpea flour
- ¼ cup water
- 2 teaspoons minced garlic
- 3 tablespoons finely chopped dill pickle
- 1 tablespoon nutritional yeast
- Fine sea salt to taste
- Pepper to taste
- Cooking spray

For serving:

- 1 green onion, thinly sliced
- 1 teaspoon chopped fresh dill
- Chopped dill pickle

Directions:

1. To make lemon garlic aioli: Add all the ingredients for aioli into a bowl and whisk well. Cover and set aside for a few minutes for the flavors to set in.
2. Place a skillet over medium heat. Add oil. When the oil is heated, add garlic and sauté until light brown.
3. Stir in carrot and dill pickle and cook for a couple of minutes. Turn off the heat.
4. Add rest of the ingredients into a bowl and whisk well. Add carrot mixture and stir. Let the batter rest for a couple of minutes.
5. Place a nonstick pan over medium heat. When the pan is heated, spray the pan with cooking spray. Pour 2 tablespoons of batter on the pan. Spread into a small round pancake of about 4 inches by swirling the pan. Slowly bubbles will appear. Cook until the underside is medium brown in color. Flip sides and cook the other side as well.
6. If your pan is big enough, then make the pancakes in batches. Keep warm the pancakes.
7. Repeat steps 5 and make pancakes with the remaining batter.
8. Serve garnished with green onion, dill, dill pickle and lemon garlic aioli.

Coconut Flour Pancakes

Number of servings: 4

Nutritional values per serving: 2 pancakes

Calories – 220, Fat – 10.5 g, Carbohydrate – 15.5 g, Fiber – 11.5 g, Protein – 17 g

Ingredients:

- 2 scoops plant based protein powder
- 4 tablespoons psyllium husk powder, soaked in a cup of water
- 2 tablespoons coconut oil
- 2 teaspoons baking powder
- ½ cup coconut flour
- 2 cups water
- 2 teaspoons vanilla extract

Directions:

1. Add vanilla and coconut oil to the bowl of psyllium husk. Mix well and set aside for a while.
2. Mix together in a large bowl, protein powder, baking powder and coconut flour.
3. Add water and mix well.
4. Add the psyllium mixture into the bowl of dry ingredients and mix until well combined.
5. Place a nonstick pan over medium heat. Pour about ¼ cup batter on it. Swirl the pan so that the batter spreads a little.
6. Cook until the underside is golden brown. Flip sides and cook the other side as well.
7. Repeat the above 2 steps with the remaining batter.

Chive Waffles with Maple & Soy Mushrooms

Number of servings: 3

Nutritional values per serving:

Calories – 227, Fat – 8 g, Carbohydrate – 30 g, Fiber – 4 g, Protein – 7 g

Ingredients:

- 1 cup soy milk or rice milk
- 1 tablespoon rape seed oil
- 2.6 ounces polenta
- ½ tablespoon baking powder
- ½ tablespoon maple syrup
- 3 large mushrooms, cut into thick slices
- Soy yogurt to serve (optional)
- ½ teaspoon apple cider vinegar or lemon juice
- 1.8 ounces mashed sweet potato
- 2.3 ounces all-purpose flour
- ½ small bunch chives, snipped
- 1 teaspoon light soy sauce
- Olive oil, to fry

Directions:

1. Whisk together in a bowl, milk, rapeseed oil and vinegar. The mixture may begin to curdle but that's ok.
2. Add sweet potato and whisk well.
3. Add all the dry ingredients into a bowl and stir.
4. Add wet ingredients into the bowl of dry ingredients and whisk well.
5. Add half the chives.
6. Pour batter into a preheated waffle iron. When the waffle is cooked brown, take out the waffle and keep warm.

7. Whisk together maple syrup and soy sauce and pour over the mushrooms. Sprinkle pepper and toss well.
8. Place a pan over medium heat. Add a little olive oil. When the oil is heated, add mushrooms and cook until tender.
9. Spoon mushrooms over the waffles. Sprinkle chives and serve with soy yogurt if desired.

Vegan Crepes

Number of servings: 4

Nutritional values per serving: 1 crepe, without toppings

Calories – 93, Fat – 1 g, Carbohydrate – 18 g, Fiber – NA, Protein – 3 g

Ingredients:

- 6 tablespoons white whole-wheat flour
- 6 tablespoons all-purpose flour
- ¾ cup + 2 tablespoons unsweetened nondairy milk
- ½ tablespoon flaxseed meal
- ¼ teaspoon sugar
- 1 ½ tablespoons water
- ¼ teaspoon salt

Directions:

1. Add all the ingredients into a blender and blend until smooth.
2. Pour into a bowl and chill for 20-30 minutes.
3. Place a nonstick (10 inch) pan over medium heat. Spray with cooking spray.
4. When the pan is heated, pour ¼ cup batter on the pan. Swirl the pan so that the batter spreads.
5. Cook until the underside is light brown. Flip sides and cook until the underside is light brown.
6. Remove crepe onto a plate.
7. Repeat steps 3-6 and make the remaining crepes.
8. Serve warm with toppings of your choice.

Chocolate Coconut Crepes

Number of servings: 2

Nutritional values per serving: 1 crepe

Calories – 203, Fat – 18 g, Carbohydrate – 15 g, Fiber – 5 g, Protein – 4 g

Ingredients:

- 2 store bought coconut wraps
- 2 tablespoons sun butter or coconut butter
- 2 ounces unsweetened baking chocolate, chopped
- 3-4 teaspoons swerve confectioners sweetener

Directions:

1. Place a pan over medium heat. When the pan heats, place the coconut wrap on it and heat the crepes on one side only for 10-15 seconds. Heating for longer time can make the wrap hard.
2. Sprinkle half the chocolate pieces over the crepe. The chocolates will begin to melt. Spread the chocolates using a spoon.
3. Sprinkle sweetener all over the crepes. Spread again using the spoon. Spoon the sun butter or coconut butter over the crepe.
4. Fold the crepe in half and fold once more into a quarter.
5. Sprinkle remaining chocolates on top and serve.
6. Repeat all the above steps and make the other crepe.

Cinnamon Sugar Crepes

Number of servings: 2

Nutritional values per serving:

Calories – 116, Fat – 10 g, Carbohydrate – 12 g, Fiber – 3 g, Protein – 1 g

Ingredients:

- 2 teaspoons ghee or coconut oil
- 2 teaspoons ground cinnamon
- 2 teaspoons Monk fruit sweetener
- 2 store bought coconut wraps

Directions:

1. Place a pan over medium heat. When the pan heats, place the coconut wrap on it and heat the crepes on one side only for 10-15 seconds. Heating for longer time can make the wrap hard.
2. Spread a teaspoon of ghee all over the wrap.
3. Scatter a teaspoon of Monk fruit sweetener. Sprinkle a teaspoon of cinnamon all over the wrap.
4. Fold the crepe in half and fold once more into a quarter.
5. Sprinkle remaining chocolates on top and serve.
6. Repeat all the above steps and make the other crepe.

Vegan Chickpea Omelette

Number of servings: 2

Nutritional values per serving:

Calories – 174, Fat – 3 g, Carbohydrate – 26 g, Fiber – 4 g, Protein – 9 g

Ingredients:

For dry ingredients:

- ½ cup chickpea flour
- ¼ teaspoon salt
- ½ tablespoon flaxseed meal or chia seed meal
- 1/8 teaspoon garlic powder
- 1/8 teaspoon ground cumin
- 1/8 teaspoon turmeric powder
- 1/8 teaspoon baking soda
- 1/8 teaspoon Himalayan pink salt

For wet ingredients:

- 6 tablespoons water
- 1 ½ tablespoons nondairy yogurt of your choice, unsweetened

For vegetables:

- 1 small red onion, sliced
- 1 tomato, sliced
- A handful fresh cilantro, chopped
- ½ jalapeño, sliced or use pickled jalapeño slices
- 2 teaspoons nutritional yeast
- Olive oil for frying

Directions:

1. Add all the dry ingredients into a bowl and stir. Whisk well. Add wet ingredients into the bowl of dry ingredients and whisk well. The batter should be of the consistency of pancake batter. So add more water if required.
2. Place a nonstick skillet over medium heat. Add a little oil. When the oil is heated, pour the batter all over the pan. Place onion, tomato and jalapeño slices all over the omelet.
3. Cook until the underside is golden brown. Flip sides and cook the other side for a couple of minutes.
4. Remove onto a plate. Sprinkle nutritional yeast on top. Cut into 2 halves and serve.

Lentil Veggie Asparagus Frittata

Number of servings: 2

Nutritional values per serving:

Calories – 210, Fat – 8 g, Carbohydrate – 24 g, Fiber – 11 g, Protein – 11 g

Ingredients:

For lentil frittata:

- ¼ cup red lentils, soaked in water for an hour
- 2 tablespoons almond meal
- 1 teaspoon arrowroot starch or cornstarch
- 1/3 teaspoon salt or to taste
- ¼ teaspoon garlic powder
- ¼ teaspoon chipotle pepper
- ¼ teaspoon cayenne pepper
- 1 tablespoon nutritional yeast
- ½ teaspoon lemon juice
- ½ cup water
- ½ tablespoon flaxseed meal or chia seed meal
- ½ teaspoon baking powder
- 1/8 teaspoon turmeric powder
- 1/8 teaspoon Himalayan pink salt or to taste
- 1 teaspoon extra-virgin olive oil
- 1 teaspoon chopped sundried tomatoes

For vegetables:

- ½ teaspoon oil
- 2 cloves garlic, minced
- 1 cup chopped vegetables (mixture of carrot, cauliflower, peas and bell peppers)
- Salt to taste

- A large pinch oregano
- A large pinch thyme
- ¼ cup chopped onion
- 2/3 cup chopped asparagus (1 inch pieces)
- ¼ cup packed baby spinach
- Chipotle pepper powder to taste
- Pepper to taste
- 2 tablespoons vegan shredded cheese (optional)

Directions:

1. Grease a small, round baking dish with oil. Place a sheet of parchment paper if desired.
2. Place a skillet over medium heat. Add oil. When the oil is heated, add onion and garlic and sauté until onion turns soft.
3. Add vegetables and stir. Cover with a lid and cook for a couple of minutes.
4. Add spinach, asparagus and spices and stir. Cover and cook for a couple of minutes.
5. Remove from heat and let the mixture remain covered for one more minute. Transfer into the prepared baking dish.
6. To make lentil mixture: Drain and place the lentils in a blender. Add water and blend until smooth.
7. Add rest of the ingredients and blend until smooth.
8. Pour the mixture into the baking dish, all over the vegetables.
9. Sprinkle vegan cheese if using.
10. Bake in a preheated oven at 350°F for about 30-40 minutes or until set. A toothpick when inserted in the center should come out clean.
11. Cut into wedges and serve.

Asparagus & Mushroom Vegan Quiche

Number of servings: 3

Nutritional values per serving: 2 wedges

Calories – 240, Fat – 7 g, Carbohydrate – 29 g, Fiber – 9 g, Protein – 21 g

Ingredients:

- 1 cup chopped asparagus
- ½ cup chopped tomato
- 6.2 ounces silken tofu
- 2 tablespoons nutritional yeast
- ½ teaspoon ground thyme
- ¼ teaspoon turmeric powder
- ½ teaspoon ground oregano
- Pepper to taste
- 4 ounces mushrooms, sliced
- 1 cup chopped kale or spinach
- ½ cup chickpea flour
- 1 tablespoon soy sauce
- ¼ teaspoon Himalayan pink salt
- Cooking spray

Directions:

1. Grease a small ovenproof skillet with cooking spray and set side.
2. Place a wok over medium heat. Spray some cooking spray in it.
3. Place asparagus in the wok and cook for 4 minutes.
4. Stir in tomatoes, kale and mushrooms and cook until tender.
5. Meanwhile, add rest of the ingredients into a blender and blend until well incorporated.

6. Transfer the vegetables from the wok into the prepared skillet. Pour the blended mixture into the skillet and stir lightly.
7. Bake in a preheated oven at 350° F for about 30-40 minutes or until set. Take out the skillet from the oven and let it rest for 10 minutes.
8. Cut into 6 equal wedges and serve.

Mexican Vegan Frittata

Number of servings: 3

Nutritional values per serving:

Calories – 194, Fat – 6g, Carbohydrate – 23 g, Fiber – 7 g, Protein – 11 g

Ingredients:

For black bean mixture:

- ½ tablespoon olive oil + extra to grease
- ½ cup chopped red pepper
- ¼ teaspoon chili powder
- 1/8 teaspoon ground cumin
- Salt to taste
- Pepper to taste
- ¼ teaspoon Mexican oregano
- 1/8 teaspoon cayenne pepper
- 1 small red onion, chopped
- 2 small cloves garlic, minced
- ½ can (from a 15 ounces can) black beans

For tofu mixture:

- 7 ounces extra-firm tofu
- Salt to taste
- Pepper to taste
- ¼ cup chopped vegan cheddar cheese

Directions:

1. To make black bean mixture: Place a pan over medium heat. Add oil. When the oil is heated, add onion and cook until pink.

2. Stir in the garlic and sauté for a few seconds until aromatic.
3. Stir in the black beans and red pepper and cook for 3-4 minutes. Add rest of the ingredients and mix well. Cook for a minute or so until aromatic. Turn off the heat.
4. To make tofu mixture: Add tofu and cheese into the food processor bowl and process until well incorporated.
5. Pour into the bowl of black beans and fold.
6. Transfer into a round, greased baking dish.
7. Bake in a preheated oven at 350° F for about 20-30 minutes or until set. Take out the skillet from the oven and let it rest for 10 minutes.
8. Cut into 6 equal wedges and serve.

Chapter Nine: Plant Based Breakfast Toast and Sandwich Recipes

Avocado and Feta Toast

Number of servings: 4

Nutritional values per serving:

Calories – 297, Fat – 21 g, Carbohydrate – 22 g, Fiber – 8 g, Protein – 9 g

Ingredients:

- 2 ripe avocadoes, peeled, pitted, mashed
- 4 slices whole wheat bread, toasted
- ½ cup feta cheese, crumbled
- Salt to taste
- Pepper to taste

Directions:

1. Beat the avocadoes with a fork until smooth.
2. Spread the avocado over the toasted bread slices. Season with salt and pepper.
3. Sprinkle feta cheese on top and serve.

Banana French toast with Caramelized Bananas

Number of servings: 6

Nutritional values per serving:

Calories – 220, Fat – 2 g, Carbohydrate – 49 g, Fiber – 3 g, Protein – 2 g

Ingredients:

For French toast batter:

- 1 large over ripe banana, sliced
- 4 tablespoons maple syrup
- 1 teaspoon vanilla extract
- ½ teaspoon ground nutmeg
- 1 cup almond milk or any other nondairy milk of your choice
- 4 tablespoons flour
- 2 teaspoons oil
- ¼ teaspoon salt
- ¼ teaspoon pepper

For caramelized bananas:

- 4 tablespoons coconut sugar or vegan brown sugar
- ½ teaspoon ground cinnamon or nutmeg
- 4 ripe bananas, sliced
- 4 tablespoons almond milk or any other nondairy milk of your choice

Other ingredients:

- 2 loaves a day old sourdough bread or rustic bread, sliced

Directions:

1. Add all the ingredients for French toast batter into a blender and blend until smooth.
2. Pour into a shallow bowl.
3. Place a skillet over medium flame. Add a teaspoon of oil and swirl the pan to spread the oil.
4. Dip a slice of bread in the batter and let it remain in the batter for 2 seconds. Flip sides and let it remain in the batter for 2 seconds. Shake to drop off excess batter and place the bread slice on the skillet. Place as many slices as can fit in the pan.
5. Lower the heat to medium-low and cook until underside is golden brown. Flip sides and cook the other side until golden brown. If the bread slices are golden brown, you may find it difficult to flip sides so wait until it is golden brown. Remove on to a plate.
6. Repeat steps 3-5 and fry the remaining bread slices. Place some caramelized bananas on top and serve.
7. Meanwhile, make the caramelized bananas as follows: Add all the ingredients of caramelized banana into a skillet. Place the skillet over medium heat. Stir occasionally and cook until the syrup is thick.

White Bean & Avocado Toast

Number of servings: 2

Nutritional values per serving:

Calories – 230, Fat – 9 g, Carbohydrate – 35 g, Fiber – 11 g, Protein – 11 g

Ingredients:

- 2 slices whole-wheat bread, toasted
- 1 cup canned white beans, rinsed, drained
- ½ cup mashed avocado
- Kosher salt to taste
- Crushed red pepper to taste
- Pepper to taste

Directions:

1. Mix together avocado and beans into a bowl and stir.
2. Spread avocado mixture over bread slices. Sprinkle salt, pepper and crushed red pepper on top and serve.

Mexi-Melt

Number of servings: 2

Nutritional values per serving:

Calories – 124, Fat – 3 g, Carbohydrate – 17 g, Fiber – 3 g, Protein – 7 g

Ingredients:

- 4 tablespoons canned, nonfat, refried beans
- 2 tablespoons salsa
- 2 slices whole wheat bread, toasted
- 2 shredded tablespoons Mexican blend or Jack cheese

Directions:

1. Smear 2 tablespoons refried beans on each toast.
2. Drizzle 1-tablespoon salsa and sprinkle cheese on top. Place on a microwave safe plate.
3. Microwave on High for 45 seconds or until cheese melts.
4. Serve immediately.

Peanut Butter-Banana Cinnamon Toast

Number of servings: 2

Nutritional values per serving:

Calories – 266, Fat – 9 g, Carbohydrate – 38 g, Fiber – 5 g, Protein – 8 g

Ingredients:

- 2 slices whole wheat bread, toasted
- 2 small bananas, sliced
- 2 tablespoons peanut butter
- Ground cinnamon to garnish

Directions:

1. Spread a tablespoon of peanut butter on each of the bread slices.
2. Place a layer of banana slices on each toast.
3. Garnish with cinnamon and serve.

Creamy Spinach Toast

Number of servings: 3

Nutritional values per serving:

Calories – 60, Fat – 2 g, Carbohydrate – 12 g, Fiber – NA, Protein – 6 g

Ingredients:

- 3 tablespoons grated mozzarella cheese
- 3 slices whole wheat bread, lightly toasted

For spinach topping:

- 4.5 ounces shredded spinach
- 2 tablespoons minced onion
- 1 teaspoon corn starch
- ¼ teaspoon baking soda
- ½ tablespoon Earth balance butter
- 1 green chili, thinly sliced
- 2 tablespoons low-fat milk
- Salt to taste
- Pepper to taste

Directions:

1. Place a nonstick pan over medium heat. Add vegan butter. When it melts, add onion and chilies and sauté until onion turns pink.
2. Stir in spinach and baking soda and cook until spinach wilts.
3. Whisk together cornstarch and milk in a bowl and pour into the pan. Stir constantly until thick. Add salt and pepper to taste. Remove from heat and let it cool completely.

4. Spread 1/3 of the spinach over each bread slice. Sprinkle cheese on top.
5. Broil in a preheated oven for a few minutes until cheese melts.
6. Serve hot.

Masala Cheese Toast

Number of servings: 2

Nutritional values per serving:

Calories – 90, Fat – 4 g, Carbohydrate – 14 g, Fiber – NA, Protein – 3 g

Ingredients:

- 2 slices whole wheat bread
- ¼ cup finely chopped, boiled, mixed vegetables (peas, cauliflower, bell pepper and cabbage)
- 1 tablespoon chopped onion
- 2 tablespoons mashed, boiled potatoes
- 1 tablespoon chopped fresh cilantro
- Salt to taste
- A pinch chili powder
- ½ green chili, sliced
- 2 tablespoons grated mozzarella cheese
- 1 teaspoon garam masala
- 1 ½ tablespoons oil

Directions:

1. Place a nonstick pan over medium heat. Add oil. When the oil is heated, add onion and green chili and stir. Cook for a minute.
2. Add vegetables, salt, spices, mashed potato and cilantro and mix well. Heat thoroughly. Let it cool for 10 minutes.
3. Toast the bread slices to the desired doneness.
4. Spread half the vegetables mixture over each bread slice. Sprinkle cheese on top.
5. Broil in an oven for a couple of minutes until cheese melts.

6. Serve hot.

Quark & Cucumber Toast

Number of servings: 2

Nutritional values per serving:

Calories – 141, Fat – 5 g, Carbohydrate – 14 g, Fiber – 2 g, Protein – 8 g

Ingredients:

- 2 slices whole-grain bread
- ¼ cup chopped cucumber
- Sea salt to taste
- ¼ cup quark cheese
- 2 tablespoons chopped cilantro leaves

Directions:

1. Toast the bread slices to the desired doneness.
2. Spread a tablespoon of quark cheese on each toast.
3. Scatter cucumber and cilantro.
4. Season with salt and serve.

Grilled Corn and Capsicum Sandwich

Number of servings: 2

Nutritional values per serving:

Calories – 160, Fat – 2 g, Carbohydrate – 30 g, Fiber – NA, Protein – 4 g

Ingredients:

- 4.2 ounces cooked corn kernels
- 2 tablespoons finely chopped onions
- 1 green chili, sliced
- Salt to taste
- Pepper to taste
- 3 tablespoons finely chopped bell peppers
- 2 large cloves garlic, peeled, minced
- 2 tablespoons butter or vegan butter

Directions:

1. Place a nonstick pan over medium heat. Add ½ tablespoon butter. When butter melts, add garlic, onion and green chili and sauté for a few seconds until aromatic.
2. Stir in the corn and bell pepper. Season with salt and pepper. Cook for a couple of minutes. Turn off the heat.
3. Divide the mixture into 2 portions and spread each portion on 1 bread slice.
4. Cover with the remaining bread slices.
5. Spread remaining butter on either side of the sandwiches.
6. Grill the sandwich until golden brown and serve.

Veggie Sandwich

Number of servings: 2

Nutritional values per serving: 1 sandwich with 1 clementine

Calories – 174, Fat – 6 g, Carbohydrate – 27 g, Fiber – 3 g, Protein – 6 g

Ingredients:

- 4 slices sprouted grain bread
- 2 tablespoons hummus
- 8 slices cucumber
- 2 tablespoons shredded carrot
- ½ avocado, peeled, pitted mashed
- Salt to taste
- 4 slices tomato
- 2 clementine's, peeled, separated into segments, deseeded

Directions:

1. Spread avocado on 2 slices of bread. Sprinkle salt over it.
2. Place tomato and cucumber slices over it. Scatter carrot on top.
3. Spread hummus on the remaining 2 bread slices. Cover the sandwiches with these slices, with the hummus side facing down.
4. Cut into desired shape and serve with clementine.

Warm Goat Cheese, Beet and Arugula Sandwiches

Number of servings: 2

Nutritional values per serving:

Calories – 261, Fat – 20 g, Carbohydrate – 13 g, Fiber – 2 g, Protein – 10 g

Ingredients:

- 1 teaspoon balsamic vinegar
- 1 ½ tablespoons olive oil
- 4 bread slices (½ inch thick) from a round country loaf
- ½ can (from a 14.5 ounces can) sliced beets, drained
- 3 ounces soft mild goat cheese, softened
- 8 large arugula leaves
- ¼ teaspoon Dijon mustard
- 2 very thin red onion slices, separate the rings
- Salt to taste
- Pepper to taste

Directions:

1. Add vinegar, salt, pepper and Dijon mustard into a bowl and stir.
2. Add 1-tablespoon oil and whisk well. Add beets and toss well.
3. Place bread slices on a baking sheet. Brush oil on top of the bread slices.
4. Sprinkle salt and pepper.
5. Set the oven to broiler mode. Place rack 6 inches away from the heating element.
6. Place baking sheet in the oven and broil for 1-2 minutes.
7. Take out 2 slices of bread from the oven and set aside. Flip the remaining 2 bread slices. Divide the goat cheese and spread it over the bread slices.

8. Broil for another minute.
9. Place beet slices, onion and arugula. Cover with the remaining 2 bread slices, with the toasted side facing up.
10. Cut into desired shape and serve.

Chapter Ten: Plant Based Breakfast Baking Recipes (Muffins, Breads, Scones, etc.)

Chocolate Muffins

Number of servings: 6

Nutritional values per serving:

Calories – 105, Fat – 1 g, Carbohydrate – 23 g, Fiber – NA, Protein – 5 g

Ingredients:

- ½ can (from a 15 ounces can) black beans, drained
- 5 tablespoons coconut palm sugar
- 2 tablespoons unsweetened applesauce
- 1 ½ tablespoons ground flaxseeds
- ½ teaspoon arrowroot powder
- 1/8 teaspoon salt or to taste
- 6 tablespoons cacao powder

- ½ small banana, sliced
- 3 tablespoons water
- ¾ teaspoon baking powder
- ½ teaspoon vanilla extract

Directions:

1. Add all the ingredients into a blender and blend until well incorporated.
2. Grease a 6 counts muffin tin with some cooking spray. Place disposable liners in it.
3. Divide the mixture among the muffin cups.
4. Bake in a preheated oven at 350°F for about 25-30 minutes or until the top is brown and cracked at a couple of places.
5. Remove from the oven and place on a wire rack to cool.
6. Remove from the muffin tin and serve.

Cherry Dark Chocolate Chip Muffins

Number of servings: 18

Nutritional values per serving:

Calories – 192, Fat – 9 g, Carbohydrate – 26 g, Fiber – 1 g, Protein – 2.5 g

Ingredients:

- ¾ cup ground oats
- 2 teaspoons baking powder
- 1 teaspoon baking soda
- ¼ teaspoon salt
- 2 cups whole wheat pastry flour or unbleached all-purpose flour
- ½ cup vegan brown sugar
- 1 ½ cups almond milk
- 2 heaping cups cherries, (first measure and pit and chop them
- ½ cup melted coconut oil or olive oil or avocado oil
- 2 teaspoons almond extract
- ½ cup chopped dairy-free dark chocolate, divided

Directions:

1. Add all the dry ingredients and brown sugar into a mixing bowl and stir.
2. Whisk together all the wet ingredients in another bowl.
3. Pour the wet ingredients into the bowl of dry ingredients and stir until just incorporated. Do not over-mix.
4. Add cherries and most of the chocolate and fold gently.
5. Grease three 6 counts muffin tins with some cooking spray. Place disposable liners in it.
6. Divide the mixture among the muffin cups.

7. Bake in a preheated oven at 350°F for about 25-30 minutes or until the top is brown and cracked at a couple of places.
8. Remove from the oven and place on a wire rack to cool.
9. Remove from the muffin tin and serve.
10. Store leftovers in an airtight container at room temperature for up to 3 days or in the refrigerator for up to 7 days.
11. Warm the muffins and serve.

Banana Nut Muffins

Number of servings: 4

Nutritional values per serving:

Calories – 370, Fat – 16 g, Carbohydrate – 50 g, Fiber – 6 g, Protein – 7 g

Ingredients:

- 1 cup whole wheat pastry flour
- A pinch salt
- 6 tablespoons vegan brown sugar
- 1 flax eggs (whisk together 1 tablespoon ground flaxseed with 3 tablespoons water and chill for 15 minutes)
- 2 over ripe bananas, mashed
- 1 teaspoon vanilla extract
- 2 tablespoons vegan butter
- ½ cup walnuts

Directions:

1. Add banana, brown sugar, baking soda and salt into a mixing bowl and whisk well.
2. Add flax egg, vanilla extract, melted vegan butter and mix.
3. Add flour and fold until just combined. Do not over-mix.
4. Grease 4 ramekins or muffin cups. Divide and pour the batter into the ramekins.
5. Sprinkle walnuts over it,
6. Bake in a preheated oven at 375 °F for about 25 to 30 minutes or a toothpick when inserted comes out clean.
7. Remove from the oven and let it cool for a while. Invert on to a plate and remove the muffins and serve warm.

Peanut Butter & Chia Berry Jam English Muffins

Number of servings: 2

Nutritional values per serving: 2 muffins

Calories – 262, Fat – 9 g, Carbohydrate – 40 g, Fiber – 9 g, Protein – 10 g

Ingredients:

- 1 cup mixed frozen berries, unsweetened
- 4 teaspoons natural peanut butter
- 4 teaspoons chia seeds
- 2 whole wheat English muffins, split

Directions:

1. Place berries in a microwave safe bowl. Microwave on High for about 2 minutes, stirring every 30 seconds.
2. Add chia seeds and mix well.
3. Spread a teaspoon of peanut butter on each muffin half. Divide the berry mixture and spread on each half.
4. Serve.

Whole Wheat Bread

Number of servings: 2 loaves

Nutritional values per serving: 1.2 ounces each slice

Calories – 84, Fat – 1.6 g, Carbohydrate – 15.1 g, Fiber – 0.6 g, Protein – 2.1 g

Ingredients:

- 4 cups bread flour
- 2 cups whole wheat flour
- 2 tablespoons vegan sugar
- 4 ½ teaspoons active dry yeast
- 2 teaspoons salt
- 4 tablespoons extra virgin olive oil
- 2 cups warm water (slightly more than Luke warm water)

Directions:

1. To a large mixing bowl, add whole-wheat flour, bread flour, sugar, salt, and yeast. Mix until well combined.
2. Gently pour olive oil and water. Mix well and knead into dough. Knead for 10 minutes either with your hands or in a food processor fitted with the dough kneading attachment on low speed.
3. Grease a bowl liberally with some oil. Place the dough in the bowl. Turn the dough around in the bowl so that the dough is coated with oil.
4. Cover the bowl loosely and keep aside for 45 minutes or until the dough doubles in size.
5. Punch the dough and divide into 2 portions. Shape into loaf and place in 2 loaf pans

6. Cover the loaf pans loosely with greased plastic wrap. Keep in a warm area for about 45 minutes or until the dough rises again.
7. Bake in a preheated oven at 450 °F for about 10 minutes.
8. Lower the temperature to 350 °F and bake for 30 minutes. Remove from the oven and let it cool on the wire rack.
9. Cut into slices of about 1.2 ounces and serve.

Blueberry Mini Muffins

Number of servings: 6

Nutritional values per serving: 2 mini muffins

Calories – 106, Fat – 5 g, Carbohydrate – 16 g, Fiber – 2 g, Protein – 1 g

Ingredients:

- ¾ cup rolled oats
- 1/8 teaspoon baking soda
- ½ teaspoon baking powder
- 1/8 teaspoon salt
- 3 tablespoons packed light brown sugar
- ½ tablespoon ground flaxseeds
- 6 tablespoons blueberries, chop if larger in size
- 1 ½ tablespoons water
- ¼ cup unsweetened applesauce
- 1 ½ tablespoons canola oil
- ½ teaspoon vanilla extract

Directions:

1. Grease a 12 counts muffin tin with cooking spray and set aside.
2. Add oats into a blender and process until finely powdered.
3. Add rest of the dry ingredients and pulse for a few seconds until well incorporated.
4. Add rest of the ingredients except blueberries and process until smooth.
5. Pour the batter into the muffin pan. Sprinkle blueberries in each cup. Stir lightly.
6. Bake in a preheated oven at 350 °F for about 25 to 30 minutes or a toothpick when inserted comes out clean.

7. Remove from the oven and let it cool for a while. Invert on to a plate and remove the muffins and serve warm.

Strawberry Banana Mini Bread Loaves / Muffins

Number of servings: 12 mini loaves or 18 muffins

Nutritional values per serving: For 1 mini loaf

Calories – 87, Fat – 3 g, Carbohydrate – 15 g, Fiber – 1 g, Protein – 1 g

Nutritional values per serving: For 1 muffin

Calories – 58, Fat – 2 g, Carbohydrate – 10 g, Fiber – 1 g, Protein – 1 g

Ingredients:

- 1/3 cup coconut milk
- 3 teaspoons chia seeds
- ½ tablespoon vanilla
- 1 ¼ teaspoons baking powder
- ½ cup finely chopped fresh strawberries
- ½ cup mashed over ripe bananas
- 1 ½ tablespoons maple syrup
- 1 tablespoon coconut oil, melted
- ½ cup + 2 tablespoons gluten- free flour blend
- ½ tablespoon ground cinnamon

Directions:

1. Add all the wet ingredients except strawberries into a large bowl and whisk well. Set aside for 5 minutes.
2. Add all the dry ingredients into another bowl and stir.
3. Add the dry ingredients into the bowl of wet ingredients and mix well.
4. Add strawberries and fold gently.

5. To make mini loaves: Grease a mini loaf tin of 12 counts with olive oil cooking spray. Divide and pour the batter into the loaf tin.
6. Bake in a preheated oven at 350° F for 10-12 minutes or a toothpick when inserted in the center of the loaf comes out clean.
7. To make muffins: Grease 3 mini muffin tins of 6 counts each with olive oil. Divide and pour the batter into the muffin tin.
8. Bake in a preheated oven at 350° F for 8-12 minutes or a toothpick when inserted in the center of the loaf comes out clean.
9. Serve warm.

Quinoa Flour Pumpkin Bread

Number of servings: 5

Nutritional values per serving: 1 slice

Calories – 215, Fat – 7 g, Carbohydrate – 35 g, Fiber – 2 g, Protein – 3 g

Ingredients:

- ¾ cup + 2 tablespoons quinoa flour
- ½ teaspoon baking soda
- ½ teaspoon baking powder
- ½ teaspoon ground cinnamon
- ¼ teaspoon salt
- ¾ teaspoon pumpkin pie spice
- ½ cup cooked or canned pumpkin puree
- ½ teaspoon vanilla extract
- 2 tablespoons apple sauce, unsweetened
- 2 tablespoons dairy free mini chocolate chips or chopped walnuts or chopped pecans (optional)
- ½ cup coconut sugar or any other unrefined granulated sugar of your choice
- 2 tablespoons coconut oil, melted
- ½ flax egg (½ tablespoon ground flaxseed mixed with 1 ½ tablespoons water)

Directions:

1. Grease a small loaf pan with cooking spray.
2. Mix together the flax egg ingredients and set aside for 15 minutes in the refrigerator.
3. Add all the wet ingredients into a bowl and whisk until well incorporated.
4. Add all the dry ingredients into another bowl and stir.

5. Add the dry ingredients into the bowl of wet ingredients and mix until just combined. Do not over-mix.
6. Spoon the batter into the prepared loaf pan. Place rack in the center of the oven.
7. Bake in a preheated oven at 350° F for about 30-40 minutes or until a toothpick when inserted in the center comes out clean.
8. Let it cool completely. Remove loaf from the pan. Cut into 5 equal slices and serve.

Pumpkin Bread

Number of servings: 6

Nutritional values per serving:

Calories – 191, Fat – 7 g, Carbohydrate – 31 g, Fiber – 3 g, Protein – 3 g

Ingredients:

- 1 flax egg (1 tablespoon ground flaxseed mixed with 3 tablespoons water)
- 6 tablespoons unsweetened almond milk
- 3 tablespoons canola oil
- ¾ cup plain pumpkin puree (canned or cooked)
- ½ teaspoon vanilla extract
- 1 cup white whole wheat flour
- ½ teaspoon pumpkin pie spice or ground cinnamon
- ¼ cup bittersweet chocolate chips (optional)
- 1 teaspoon baking powder
- ¼ teaspoon salt

Directions:

1. Grease a small loaf pan with cooking spray (you can use a disposable loaf pan).
2. After mixing the flax meal and water, place in the refrigerator for 15 minutes.
3. Add all the wet ingredients (including flax egg) into a mixing bowl and whisk well.
4. Add all the dry ingredients into another bowl and stir. Add the dry ingredients into the bowl of wet ingredients and mix until just combined. Do not over-mix.
5. Spoon the batter into the prepared loaf pan. Place rack in the center of the oven.

6. Bake in a preheated oven at 350° F for about 30-40 minutes or until a toothpick when inserted in the center comes out clean.
7. Let it cool completely. Remove loaf from the pan. Cut into 6 equal slices and serve.

Banana Apple Chunk Bread

Number of servings: 5

Nutritional values per serving:

Calories – 147, Fat – 0.7 g, Carbohydrate – 33.9 g, Fiber – 3.4 g, Protein – 2.4 g

Ingredients:

- 1 very ripe banana, mashed
- ¼ cup sucanat
- ¼ cup apple sauce
- ½ teaspoon salt
- ½ tablespoon chopped walnuts (optional)
- ½ apple, peeled, cored, chopped
- ¾ cup + 2 tablespoons whole wheat flour
- ½ teaspoon baking soda
- ½ teaspoon ground cinnamon

Directions:

1. Grease a small loaf pan with cooking spray (you can use a disposable loaf pan).
2. Add all the ingredients into a mixing bowl and stir until well incorporated.
3. Grease a small loaf pan with cooking spray (you can also use a disposable loaf pan).
4. Pour batter into the loaf pan.
5. Place rack in the center of the oven.
6. Bake in a preheated oven at 350° F for about 30-40 minutes or until a toothpick when inserted in the center comes out clean.
7. Let it cool completely. Remove loaf from the pan. Cut into 5 equal slices and serve.

Strawberry Breakfast Cake

Number of servings: 7

Nutritional values per serving: 1 slice

Calories – 171, Fat – 7 g, Carbohydrate – 25 g, Fiber – NA, Protein – 4 g

Ingredients:

For cake:

- 1 cup oat flour
- ½ tablespoon chia seeds
- ¼ teaspoon salt
- ½ cup almond flour
- 1 teaspoon baking powder
- ¼ cup maple syrup
- ½ teaspoon vanilla extract
- ½ cup roughly chopped fresh strawberries
- ½ teaspoon grated lemon zest
- ¼ cup almond milk
- ½ teaspoon almond extract

For frosting:

- ½ cup cashews, soaked in water for 2-3 hours
- 2 tablespoons almond milk
- ½ teaspoon vanilla extract
- 3 tablespoons maple syrup
- ¼ cup diced strawberries, divided

Directions:

1. Place a sheet of parchment paper in a small baking pan of about 6 x 6 inches. Spray some cooking spray over it.
2. Add all the dry ingredients into a bowl.

3. Add rest of the ingredients except strawberries and mix until well incorporated.
4. Add strawberries and fold gently.
5. Pour batter into the loaf pan.
6. Place rack in the center of the oven.
7. Bake in a preheated oven at 350° F for about 30-40 minutes or until a toothpick when inserted in the center comes out clean.
8. Let it cool completely. Remove loaf from the pan and place on a serving platter.
9. Meanwhile make the frosting as follows: Set aside 2 tablespoons of strawberries and add rest of the ingredients for frosting into a blender and blend until smooth.
10. Transfer into a bowl. Add remaining strawberries and stir. Spread over the cake.
11. Cut into 7 equal slices and serve.

Protein-Packed Breakfast Brownies

Number of servings: 12

Nutritional values per serving:

Calories – 145, Fat – 7.6 g, Carbohydrate – 15.3 g, Fiber – 1.8 g, Protein – 5.1 g

Ingredients:

- ½ cup white whole wheat flour
- 1 scoop plant based protein powder
- ½ teaspoon salt
- 1 cup quick cooking oats
- 2 tablespoons unsweetened cocoa powder
- ½ teaspoon baking soda
- 6 tablespoons vegan brown sugar
- 1 flax egg (1 tablespoon flaxseed meal mixed with 3 tablespoons water)
- 1/3 cup canola oil
- ½ teaspoon vanilla extract
- 1/3 cup applesauce
- ½ tablespoon mini semi-sweet chocolate chips
- 1 tablespoon chopped nuts

Directions:

1. Set aside the flaxseed meal mixture in the refrigerator for 15 minutes.
2. Place a sheet of parchment paper in a small baking pan of about 6 x 6 inches. Spray some cooking spray over it.
3. Add all the dry ingredients into a bowl and stir.
4. Add all the wet ingredients (including flax egg) into a mixing bowl and whisk well.

5. Add the dry ingredients into the bowl of wet ingredients and mix until just combined. Do not over-mix.
6. Sprinkle nuts and chocolate chips. Press lightly the nuts and chocolate chips into the batter.
7. Spoon the batter into the prepared baking pan. Place rack in the center of the oven.
8. Bake in a preheated oven at 350° F for about 15-20 minutes or until a toothpick when inserted in the center comes out clean.
9. Let it cool completely.
10. Cut into 12 equal squares and serve.

Pineapple Scones

Number of servings: 4

Nutritional values per serving:

Calories – 235, Fat – 8 g, Carbohydrate – 39 g, Fiber – NA, Protein – 6 g

Ingredients:

- 1 ½ cups whole wheat flour
- ½ teaspoon baking soda
- ½ tablespoon baking powder
- ¼ teaspoon salt
- 6 tablespoons nondairy milk of your choice
- 3 tablespoons coconut oil, frozen
- ½ can crushed pineapple, drained
- ½ tablespoon coconut sugar or brown sugar
- ½ tablespoon minced fresh rosemary
- ½ teaspoon lemon juice
- 1 ½ tablespoons maple syrup
- ½ teaspoon vanilla extract

- 1 tablespoon sliced almonds
- Cooking spray

Directions:

1. Add all the dry ingredients into a bowl and stir.
2. Add lemon juice and milk into another bowl and set aside for a few minutes. It will curdle. Stir in maple syrup.
3. Chop the frozen coconut oil into small pieces. Add into the bowl of dry ingredients. Cut it into the mixture with a pastry cutter or with your hands until crumbly in texture.
4. Add the milk mixture, a little at a time and mix each time.
5. Stir in the pineapple and vanilla. Mix until dough is formed.
6. Dust your countertop with some flour. Place the dough on your countertop and shape into a ball.
7. Flatten the dough until it is a rectangle of 2 inches in thickness. Fold the dough into a quarter (first fold in half and fold once more in half).
8. Now roll the dough until it is 1 ½ inches thick rectangle.
9. Cut into circles or 4 triangles. If cutting into circles collect the scrap dough and re-roll the dough. Repeat step 7-9 and make more circles. You should have 4 circles or triangles in all. Place the scones on a baking sheet lined with parchment paper.
10. Spray some cooking spray over the scones. Scatter coconut sugar, almonds and rosemary.
11. Place rack in the center of the oven.
12. Bake in a preheated oven at 425° F for about 10-15- minutes or until puffed up and golden brown.
13. Let it cool for a few minutes on a wire rack and serve.

Garlicky Cheddar Biscuits with Sausage Gravy

Number of servings: 3

Nutritional values per serving: 2 biscuits with 1/3-cup gravy

Calories – 366, Fat – 11g, Carbohydrate – 59 g, Fiber – NA g, Protein – 9 g

Ingredients:

For biscuits:

- 1 tablespoon lemon juice
- 6 tablespoons unsweetened soy milk or almond milk
- 1 cup all-purpose flour
- ½ tablespoon baking powder
- 1/8 teaspoon cayenne powder
- ½ tablespoon organic cane sugar
- 1 teaspoon garlic powder
- ¾ cup shredded vegan cheddar cheese
- ¼ cup vegan butter, frozen

For garlic topping:

- 1 ½ tablespoons vegan butter, melted
- ½ teaspoon garlic powder
- 1 teaspoon dried parsley

For gravy:

- 1 tablespoon olive oil
- 1 medium onion, chopped
- ¾ cup unsweetened nondairy milk of your choice
- ¼ teaspoon pepper
- 1 vegan sausage, ground or finely chopped
- 1 clove garlic, minced
- ½ teaspoon salt or to taste

- 1 tablespoon all-purpose flour
- 1/8 teaspoon chili powder

For garnishing:

- 2 tablespoons chopped fresh parsley or chives

Directions:

1. To make biscuits: Place a sheet of parchment paper on a baking sheet.
2. Add all the dry ingredients into a bowl and stir.
3. Add lemon juice and milk into another bowl and set aside for a few minutes. It will curdle.
4. Chop the frozen vegan butter into small pieces. Add into the bowl of dry ingredients. Cut it into the mixture with a pastry cutter or with your hands until crumbly in texture. Add cheese and mix well.
5. Add the milk mixture, a little at a time and mix each time. You will have a moist mixture.
6. Divide the mixture into 6 equal portions and shape into balls. Place on a baking sheet lined with parchment paper. Leave gap between the biscuits.
7. Place rack in the center of the oven.
8. Bake in a preheated oven at 425° F for about 10-15-minutes or until puffed up and dry on top and light brown on the underside.
9. To make garlic topping: Add butter, garlic powder and parsley into a bowl and stir.
10. Brush this mixture on the hot biscuits once it's ready.
11. Meanwhile, make the gravy as follows: Place a skillet over medium flame. Add oil. When the oil is heated, add onion and sausages and cook until sausages are brown.

12. Stir in garlic and cook for a minute or so until aromatic.
13. Scatter flour over the sausage and mix until well incorporated.
14. Add milk, stirring simultaneously. Lower the heat to low heat and simmer for 6-7 minutes.
15. Add seasonings and stir. Simmer for a few more minutes until thick in consistency.
16. To serve: Place 2 biscuits on each plate. Drizzle 1/3-cup gravy over the biscuits. Garnish with chives and serve.

Easy Pumpkin Spice Bagels

Number of servings: 8

Nutritional values per serving:

Calories – 164, Fat – 1 g, Carbohydrate – 34 g, Fiber – 4 g, Protein – 5 g

Ingredients:

- 2 ½ cups self-rising flour preferably whole-wheat
- 1 teaspoon pumpkin pie spice + extra to garnish
- 2 cups pumpkin puree
- 2 teaspoons melted coconut oil

Directions:

1. Add flour into a mixing bowl. Add pumpkin puree, oil and pumpkin pie spice into bowl. Fit the stand mixer with dough hook attachment.
2. Set the mixer on low speed and mix until smooth dough is formed. Add a little water if required (if the dough is too dry), a tablespoon at a time and mix each time.
3. Place rack in the upper third position in the oven. Place a sheet of parchment paper on a large baking sheet.
4. Roll the dough between your hands into a log. Divide into 8 equal portions.
5. Roll each portion into a log of about 9-10 inches and shape into bagel. Place the bagels on the prepared baking sheet.
6. Brush some oil over the bagels. Dust with pumpkin pie spice.
7. Bake in a preheated oven at 375° F for about 10-15-minutes or until light brown and dry on top and well browned on the underside.

8. Remove the baking sheet from the oven and let it cool to room temperature.
9. Serve.

Chapter Eleven: Plant Based Breakfast Sausages

Classic Breakfast Links

Number of servings: 24

Nutritional values per serving: 1 link

Calories – 50, Fat – NA, Carbohydrate – 8 g, Fiber – NA, Protein – 5 g

Ingredients:

- 2 cans (15 ounces each) pinto beans, drained, rinsed
- 4 tablespoons chickpea flour
- 2 teaspoons onion powder
- 1 teaspoon dried rosemary
- 1 tablespoon tomato paste
- 2 tablespoons water
- ½ cup vital wheat gluten
- ½ cup finely chopped mushrooms
- 1 teaspoon fennel
- 1 teaspoon dried sage
- 1 teaspoon dried rosemary
- 2 teaspoons onion powder
- 2 teaspoons maple syrup
- Salt to taste
- Pepper to taste
- Oil to fry, as required

Directions:

1. Add pinto beans into a bowl and mash well with a fork.
2. Add remaining ingredients and stir until well combined. Divide the mixture into 24 equal portions and shape into sausage links.

3. Place a skillet over medium heat. Add about a tablespoon of oil. When the oil is heated, place a few links in the pan and cook until brown all over.
4. Repeat the previous step and cook the other sausage links.
5. Serve. If you wish to store them, cook until light brown. Cool completely and transfer into an airtight container. Refrigerate until use. It can last for 3-4 days or place in a freezer safe bag and freeze for about a month.

Chickpea Hemp Seed Sausages

Number of servings: 10

Nutritional values per serving:

Calories – 85, Fat – 3.9 g, Carbohydrate – 9.4 g, Fiber – 2.5 g, Protein – 4.3 g

Ingredients:

- ½ can (from a 15 ounces can) pinto beans, drained, rinsed
- 5 tablespoons chickpea flour (garbanzo bean flour)
- ½ tablespoon vegan Worcestershire sauce
- ½ cup shelled hemp seeds
- 1 tablespoon ground flax seeds or ground chia seeds
- 1 tablespoon pure maple syrup
- 1 tablespoon dried parsley
- ½ teaspoon dried thyme
- 1 tablespoon dried oregano
- 1 teaspoon garlic powder
- ¾ teaspoon smoked paprika
- ½ teaspoon chili powder
- 1/8 teaspoon cayenne pepper (optional)
- ¾ teaspoon ground cumin
- ½ teaspoon salt or to taste
- ½ teaspoon pepper or to taste
- ½ teaspoon olive oil
- ½ teaspoon liquid smoke
- ½ cup boiling hot water

Directions:

1. Place spices and Worcestershire sauce in a bowl. Pour boiling hot water over it. Stir and set aside.

2. Add 4 tablespoons chickpea flour, flaxseed meal and hemp seeds into a bowl and stir.
3. Place a skillet over medium heat. Add oil. When the oil is heated, add the beans and spice mixture. Heat thoroughly, mashing simultaneously.
4. Add remaining chickpea flour and mix well. Heat thoroughly. Turn off the heat. Transfer the mixture into the bowl of chickpea flour. Mix until well incorporated.
5. Cool completely and refrigerate for 2-3 hours.
6. Divide the mixture into 10 equal portions and shape into patties. Place on a parchment sheet lined baking sheet.
7. Bake in a preheated oven at 375° F for about 10-15. Flip sides and bake the other side for 10-15 minutes.
8. Remove from the pan and serve hot. Cool the leftovers completely and transfer into an airtight container. It can last for 4 days or place in the freezer for 2 months. To serve, place the sausages in a heat pan with a spray of cooking spray.

Homemade Vegan Sausages

Number of servings: 8

Nutritional values per serving: 1 sausage

Calories – 123, Fat – 2 g, Carbohydrate – 7 g, Fiber – 1 g, Protein – 18 g

Ingredients:

- 1 tablespoon canola oil
- 2 cloves garlic, chopped
- 1 teaspoon fennel seeds
- 2 tablespoons tomato paste
- 1 teaspoon cumin seeds
- 1 large white onion, chopped
- ½ cup cooked chickpeas
- ¼ teaspoon salt or to taste
- 1 teaspoon smoked paprika
- ½ cup water
- 1 teaspoon dried thyme
- 2 tablespoons soy sauce
- 1 ½ cups vital wheat gluten

Directions:

1. Place a pan over medium heat. Add oil. When the oil is heated, add onion and garlic and sauté until onion turns translucent.
2. Stir in the cumin and fennel seeds. Cook until aromatic. Turn off the heat.
3. Add chickpeas, onion mixture, thyme, soy sauce, tomato paste, salt, paprika and water into the food processor bowl. Process until well incorporated.
4. Add vital wheat gluten and process until dough is formed.

5. Place a pot half filled with water and bring to a boil over high heat. When it begins to boil, lower the heat and let the water simmer.
6. Divide the sausage mixture into 8 equal portions and shape each into a log like sausage.
7. Wrap each sausage in parchment paper and then wrap in foil. Twist and seal both the ends and place sausages in a steaming basket.
8. Place the steaming basket in the simmering water. Cover the pot and let the sausages cook for 40 minutes. Flip sides half way through steaming.
9. Remove from the pot and let it cool for some time. Discard the foil and parchment paper.
10. Use as required. Store leftovers in an airtight container. It can last for 4 days in the refrigerator and for 2 months in the freezer.

Vegetarian "Sausage" Patties

Number of servings: 4

Nutritional values per serving:

Calories – 195, Fat – 8 g, Carbohydrate – 24.8 g, Fiber – 4 g, Protein – 7.9 g

Ingredients:

- ½ cup lentils, rinsed, soaked in water for an hour, drained
- 1 clove garlic, chopped
- Salt to taste
- ¼ cup rolled oats
- 1 tablespoon maple syrup
- ½ teaspoon fennel seeds
- 2 tablespoons olive oil

- 1 cup water
- 1 small onion, coarsely chopped
- 4 ounces brown mushrooms, quartered
- 1 tablespoon ground flaxseeds
- ½ teaspoon dried sage
- Freshly ground pepper to taste

Directions:

1. Pour water into a saucepan. Place the saucepan over medium-high heat. Add lentils, onion, salt to taste and garlic and bring to a boil.
2. Lower the heat to medium-low and cook until lentils are soft. Do not cover while cooking. Turn off the heat. Drain off any excess liquid from the saucepan.
3. In the meantime, add mushrooms into the food processor and pulse until finely chopped.
4. When the lentils are cooked, add lentils, oats, maple syrup, flaxseed, fennel, sage and salt to taste into the blender with mushrooms in it. Process until the mixture is coarse in texture.
5. Transfer into a bowl. Divide the mixture into 4 equal portions and shape into patties.
6. Place a large nonstick pan over medium heat. Add oil. When the oil is heated, place patties in the pan and cook until the underside is brown. Flip sides and cook the other side until golden brown.
7. Serve hot or use as required.

Vegan 'Bacon'

Number of servings: 32 slices

Nutritional values per serving:

Calories – 15, Fat – 1 g, Carbohydrate – 1 g, Fiber – 0.4 g, Protein – 0.2 g

Ingredients:

- 3 tablespoons olive oil
- 2 tablespoons vegan Worcestershire sauce
- 2 teaspoons smoked paprika
- 1 large eggplant
- 2 tablespoons olive oil
- 1 tablespoon maple syrup
- ½ teaspoon ground cumin

Directions:

1. Cut the eggplant into 2 halves lengthwise. Then cut each half into 16 strips of ¼ inch thickness.
2. Place a sheet of parchment paper in each of 3 baking sheets.
3. Place eggplant slices on the baking sheets.
4. Add rest of the ingredients into a bowl and whisk well. Brush this mixture on either side of the eggplant slices.
5. Bake in a preheated oven at 250° F for about 45 to 50 minutes. Flip sides half way through baking.

Chapter Twelve: Plant Based Breakfast Recipes with Beans and Lentils

Gigantes Plaki (Greek Baked Beans)

Number of servings: 2

Nutritional values per serving:

Calories – 276, Fat – 10 g, Carbohydrate – 26.4 g, Fiber – 10.4 g, Protein – 15 g

Ingredients:

- ½ tablespoon extra-virgin olive oil
- 2 cloves garlic, finely chopped
- 1 can (14.5 ounces) chopped tomatoes
- A pinch dried oregano
- 2.2 ounces feta cheese, crumbled
- ½ can (from a 23.2 ounces can) large butter beans
- 1 tablespoon chopped flat-leaf parsley
- 1 small onion, finely chopped
- ½ tablespoon tomato puree

- ¼ teaspoon ground cinnamon
- 2 sourdough slices, toasted

Directions:

1. Place an ovenproof skillet over medium heat. Add oil. When the oil is heated, add onion and garlic and sauté for a couple of minutes.
2. Add a bit of salt and sauté until onion turns translucent.
3. Add tomato puree and stir for about 50-60 seconds.
4. Stir in beans, tomatoes, oregano and cinnamon and mix well. Turn off the heat and transfer the skillet into an oven.
5. Bake in a preheated oven at 320° F for about 25 minutes or until thick. Stir occasionally.
6. Toast the sourdough bread slices if desired.
7. Sprinkle feta and parsley over the beans and serve along with sourdough bread slices.

Sweet Potato, Chickpea, and Quinoa Veggie Burger

Number of servings:

Nutritional values per serving: 1 burger with 1 roasted pepper slice, without bun

Calories – 202, Fat – 6.1 g, Carbohydrate – 29.6 g, Fiber – 5.8 g, Protein – 7 g

Ingredients:

- 2 small sweet potatoes
- ½ cup dry barley
- 4 tablespoons chopped parsley
- 3 teaspoons ground cumin
- 1 teaspoon pepper or to taste
- ¼ cup olive oil
- 2 cans (15 ounce each) garbanzo beans, rinsed, drained
- ½ cup quinoa
- 1 teaspoon cayenne pepper
- 1 teaspoon salt or to taste
- ¼ cup whole wheat flour
- 3 red bell peppers, quartered

Directions:

1. Place sweet potatoes and red peppers on a baking sheet.
2. Roast in a preheated oven at 400° F for about 40-60 minutes or until soft.
3. Remove the red peppers after 15 minutes or roasting and continue baking the sweet potatoes for about 45 minutes or until cooked. Remove from the oven and cool.
4. Meanwhile, cook barley and quinoa in separate pans, following the directions on the package.

5. Add sweet potatoes, garbanzo beans, parsley, cayenne pepper, cumin, salt, pepper, flour and about 2 tablespoons oil to a food processor. Pulse until you get a crumbly mixture.
6. Transfer into a large bowl. Add cooked quinoa and barley. Mix well.
7. Divide the mixture into 8 portions. Using your hands, form into patties of about 4 inches diameter.
8. Place a nonstick pan over medium heat. Add about a tablespoon of oil. Cook the patties in batches. Cook until the underside is golden brown. Flip sides and cook the other side until golden brown. Add oil to each batch of burgers.
9. Place the patty with a piece of roasted pepper and serve as it is or over buns.

Baked Beans

Number of servings: 2

Nutritional values per serving: Without bacon and serving options

Calories – 190, Fat – 3.2 g, Carbohydrate – 26.7 g, Fiber – 6.2 g, Protein – 13.9 g

Ingredients:

For tempeh bacon: Optional

Ingredients:

- 2 ounces tempeh, chopped
- ½ teaspoon maple syrup or agave nectar
- 1/8 teaspoon ground cumin
- ½ teaspoon tamari or soy sauce
- 1/8 teaspoon red hot sauce or paprika
- A little oil to fry

For baked beans:

- 1 clove garlic, minced
- ½ tablespoon maple syrup or agave nectar
- Pepper to taste
- ½ can (from a 15 ounces can) cannellini beans
- 1 small red onion, chopped
- ½ tablespoon tamari or soy sauce
- ¼ cup tomato puree
- A little oil to cook

Directions:

1. To make tempeh bacon: Set aside the tempeh and add rest of the ingredients into a bowl and mix well.

2. Place tempeh in the mixture for a couple of minutes.
3. Place a pan over medium-high heat. Add a little oil. When the oil is heated, place the tempeh in the pan and cook until underside is golden brown and crisp. Flip sides and cook the other side until golden brown and crisp.
4. Remove tempeh bacon with a slotted spoon and place on a plate lined with paper towels.
5. To make baked beans: Place the skillet back over medium heat. Add oil. When the oil is heated, add onion and garlic and cook until light golden brown.
6. Add maple syrup, tomato puree, pepper and soy sauce and mix well. Simmer for a couple of minutes.
7. Stir in the beans. Add the bacon and beans and cook until thick. Stir frequently.
8. You can also use any other type of vegan bacon.
9. Serve as it is or with toast or a part of full English breakfast.

Quick Breakfast Quinoa and Black Bean Vegan Chili

Number of servings: 8

Nutritional values per serving:

Calories – 343, Fat – 8.8 g, Carbohydrate – 44.3 g, Fiber – 12.8 g, Protein – 15.2 g

Ingredients:

- 2 onions, chopped
- 2 red chilies, chopped
- 4 teaspoons ground cumin
- 1 teaspoon chili powder or to taste (optional)
- 5 cups vegetable stock
- 2 cans (14.1 ounces each) black beans, rinsed, drained
- A handful fresh cilantro leaves, chopped
- 4 cloves garlic crushed
- 2 teaspoons hot smoked paprika
- 14.1 ounces quinoa, rinsed, drained
- 2 cans (14.1 ounces each) chopped tomatoes
- 1 medium avocado, peeled, pitted, diced
- Salt to taste
- Cooking spray

Directions:

1. Place a soup pot over medium heat. Spray some cooking spray in it.
2. Add onion and garlic and sauté for a couple of minutes. Add red chili and sauté until onion turns translucent.
3. Add all the spices and sauté for 5-6 seconds.
4. Stir in quinoa, beans, vegetable stock, salt and tomatoes.
5. Cover with a lid and lower the heat. Cook until quinoa is soft and chili is thick. Stir often.

6. Ladle into bowls. Garnish with avocado and cilantro and serve.

Veggie Vegan Breakfast Skillet

Number of servings: 2

Nutritional values per serving:

Calories – 497, Fat – 1.7 g, Carbohydrate – 97.7 g, Fiber – 19.5 g, Protein – 24.1 g

Ingredients:

- ½ can (from a 15 ounces can) pinto beans
- ½ small yellow onion, chopped
- 2 yellow potatoes, scrubbed, cut into bite size chunks
- 1 small zucchinis, chopped into bite size pieces
- 1 cup lightly packed spinach
- ½ tablespoon minced garlic
- 2 crimini mushrooms, chopped
- ½ red bell pepper, cut into bite size pieces
- 1 small carrot, cubed
- 2 tablespoons vegetable broth or water
- ½ teaspoon ground cumin
- ¼ teaspoon dried basil
- ½ teaspoon smoked paprika
- 1/8 teaspoon cayenne pepper or to taste (optional)
- 1/8 teaspoon pepper

Directions:

1. Place potatoes in a bowl. Sprinkle pepper and basil over it and toss well.
2. Transfer onto a lined baking sheet.
3. Roast in a preheated oven at 320° F for about 25-30 minutes or until potatoes are fork tender.
4. Place a skillet over medium-high heat. Add broth, onion and garlic and sauté until soft.

5. Add rest of the vegetables, potato, all the spices and beans and mix well. Cook for 10-12 minutes or until the vegetables are tender.
6. Serve hot.

Polenta and Beans

Number of servings: 3

Nutritional values per serving: 4 slices polenta with 1/3 of the bean mixture

Calories – 284, Fat – 1.8 g, Carbohydrate – 56.7 g, Fiber – 10.4 g, Protein – 11.1 g

Ingredients:

- ½ teaspoon olive oil
- 1 clove garlic, peeled, minced
- 13 ounces Pomi chopped tomatoes
- 1 cup frozen corn
- Salt to taste
- Pepper to taste
- 1 tube polenta
- ½ can (from a 15 ounces can) black beans, rinsed, drained
- ½ red bell pepper, diced
- ¼ teaspoon cayenne pepper

Directions:

1. Place a pan over medium heat. Add oil and let the pan heat.
2. Cut the polenta into ½ inch thick slices. You should have 12 slices in all. Place polenta slices in the heated pan. Cook until the underside is light brown. Flip sides and cook the other side until light brown.
3. Meanwhile, add rest of the ingredients into a saucepan. Place the saucepan over medium heat and simmer for 12-15 minutes. Stir occasionally.

4. Remove polenta from the pan and place in 3 plates. Place 1/3 of the bean mixture over the polenta and serve.

Breakfast Chickpeas with Cucumber

Number of servings: 2

Nutritional values per serving:

Calories – 225, Fat – 11.6 g, Carbohydrate – 28 g, Fiber – 6 g, Protein – 9 g

Ingredients:

For dressing:

- 3 teaspoons extra-virgin olive oil
- Freshly ground pepper to taste
- 3 teaspoons red wine vinegar
- Kosher salt to taste

For chickpeas:

- 1 cup canned chickpeas, drained
- 4 kalamata olives, pitted, finely chopped
- ¼ cup crumbled feta cheese
- ½ cup thinly sliced roasted red bell peppers
- 1 cup thinly sliced cucumber
- 4 teaspoons chopped fresh dill

Directions:

1. Add all the ingredients for dressing into a bowl and toss well.
2. Add olives, bell pepper and chickpeas and toss well.
3. Divide into plates. Sprinkle feta cheese and dill on top and serve.

Chapter Thirteen: Plant Based Breakfast Casserole Recipes

Quinoa and Broccoli Casserole

Number of servings: 2

Nutritional values per serving:

Calories – 313, Fat – 4.4 g, Carbohydrate – 57.7 g, Fiber – 6.6 g, Protein – 11.3 g

Ingredients:

- ½ cup almond milk
- 1 cup vegetable broth
- ¼ teaspoon dried thyme
- ¼ teaspoon dried oregano
- ¼ teaspoon ground nutmeg
- 0 tablespoons dried tomatoes
- ½ cup water
- ½ teaspoon nutritional yeast
- ¼ cup rice flour
- 1 ½ cups broccoli florets
- ½ cup quinoa
- Salt to taste

Directions:

1. Add ¼ cup almond milk and broth into a saucepan. Place the saucepan over medium heat. Let it come to a boil.
2. Whisk together in a bowl remaining milk, flour and all the spices and pour into the saucepan.
3. Stir constantly until thick. Turn off the heat. Add ½ cup water and nutritional yeast and whisk well. Add quinoa and stir.

4. Transfer into a greased baking dish.
5. Bake in a preheated oven at 390° F for about 30 minutes.
6. Meanwhile, place dried tomatoes in a bowl. Pour boiling water over it. Let it sit for 20 minutes. Drain and set aside.
7. Steam the broccoli until crisp as well as tender. Rinse until cold running water. Drain and set aside.
8. Chop the rehydrated tomatoes and scatter over the quinoa layer.
9. Scatter broccoli on top and serve.

Carrot and Quinoa Protein Bake

Number of servings: 4

Nutritional values per serving:

Calories – 165, Fat – 2.5 g, Carbohydrate – 26 g, Fiber – 3.5 g, Protein – 9.5 g

Ingredients:

- 1 cup grated carrots
- 1 cup unsweetened almond milk
- 2 teaspoons ground cinnamon
- ¼ teaspoon salt
- 1 cup quinoa flakes
- 2 teaspoons grated orange zest
- 2/3 cup unsweetened applesauce
- 8 packets stevia or truvia or to taste
- 3 tablespoons vanilla brown rice protein powder

Directions:

1. Grease a ceramic baking dish with cooking spray.
2. Add all the ingredients into a bowl and whisk well.
3. Add quinoa flakes and stir until well combined.
4. Spoon into the prepared baking dish.
5. Microwave on high for 7-8 minutes or until center is set.

Pumpkin Spice Latte Quinoa Breakfast Casserole

Number of servings: 2

Nutritional values per serving:

Calories – 197, Fat – 12.1 g, Carbohydrate – 20.3 g, Fiber – 2.2 g, Protein – 3.3 g

Ingredients:

- 1/3 cup warm water
- 1 tablespoon canned pumpkin puree
- ½ teaspoon melted coconut oil
- ½ teaspoon pumpkin pie spice
- 3 tablespoons warm brewed coffee
- ½ tablespoon maple syrup
- 1/8 teaspoon pure vanilla extract
- 2 tablespoons quinoa

For topping:

- 2 tablespoons raw pecans, chopped
- 1 tablespoon maple syrup
- ¼ teaspoon ground cinnamon
- ½ tablespoon coconut oil
- 1 tablespoon almond flour
- ½ tablespoon coconut flour
- A small pinch salt

Directions:

1. Add all the ingredients for casserole except quinoa into a small casserole dish and whisk well.
2. Add quinoa and stir. Cover the dish.

3. Bake in a preheated oven at 350° F for about 30 minutes or until quinoa is cooked and there is some liquid remaining in the dish.
4. Add all the topping ingredients into a bowl and mix until crumbly. Place in the freezer for a while.
5. Sprinkle the mixture over the quinoa bake. Do not cover the dish.
6. Bake until the top is brown.

Breakfast Hash Casserole with Butternut Squash & Cilantro

Number of servings: 6

Nutritional values per serving:

Calories – 170, Fat – 9 g, Carbohydrate – 22 g, Fiber – NA, Protein – 22 g

Ingredients:

- 4 tablespoons extra-virgin olive oil
- 4 cups diced zucchini
- Fine sea salt to taste
- 3 cups chopped onion
- 6 cups shredded butternut squash
- ½ cup chopped cilantro

Directions:

1. Place a skillet over medium heat. Add oil. When the oil is heated, add onions and sauté until pink
2. Lower the heat to medium –low. Stir in butternut squash, zucchini and salt and mix well.
3. Cover and cook until tender. Garnish with cilantro and serve.

Sausage-Flavored Breakfast Beans and Grits

Number of servings: 2

Nutritional values per serving:

Calories – 338, Fat – 1.5 g, Carbohydrate – 66.6 g, Fiber – 12.2 g, Protein – 16.5 g

Ingredients:

- 1 medium onion, chopped
- Water or vegetable broth, as required
- 2 cloves garlic, peeled, minced
- ½ cup vegetable broth + extra as required
- ½ teaspoon dried oregano
- ½ teaspoon rubbed sage
- ¼ teaspoon dried basil
- ½ teaspoon smoked paprika
- ¼ teaspoon fennel seeds, crushed
- ¼ teaspoon salt or to taste
- A pinch baking soda
- ¼ large red bell pepper, deseeded, chopped
- 1 ½ cups cooked or canned cannellini beans or any other variety of white beans of your choice, rinsed, drained
- ¼ teaspoon red pepper flakes or to taste
- Smoked salt to taste
- 2 cups chopped fresh spinach
- ½ cup yellow corn grits

Directions:

1. Place a nonstick skillet over medium heat. Add a tablespoon of broth or water and let the pan heat.
2. Add onion and baking soda and sauté until onion turns translucent.

3. Sprinkle more water or broth if the onions are getting stuck to the pan.
4. Add garlic and bell pepper. Sprinkle some more broth and cook for a couple of minutes until bell peppers are slightly tender. Sprinkle broth whenever necessary.
5. Add beans, all the spices and broth and stir.
6. Lower the heat and cover with a lid. Cook until thick (about 20-30 minutes). Add spinach and cook until it wilts.
7. Meanwhile, follow the instructions on the package and cook the grits.
8. Divide grits into 2 bowls. Divide the beans equally and spoon over the grits.
9. Serve hot.

Chapter Fourteen: Plant Based Breakfast Soup Recipes

Turmeric Chickpea Vegetable Soup

Number of servings: 3

Nutritional values per serving:

Calories – 100, Fat – 5g, Carbohydrate – NA g, Fiber – 2 g, Protein – 2 g

Ingredients:

- 1 tablespoon olive oil
- 1 carrot, chopped
- ½ red bell peppers, deseeded, chopped
- 1 ½ cups small cauliflower florets
- ½ teaspoon grated fresh ginger
- ½ teaspoon salt or to taste
- A pinch cayenne pepper
- ½ can (from a 15 ounces can) chickpeas, rinsed, drained
- 1 small yellow onion, chopped

- 1 celery rib, chopped
- 2 cloves garlic, minced
- 2 small bay leaves
- ½ teaspoon turmeric powder
- ¼ teaspoon paprika
- 3 cups vegetable broth
- ¾ cup chopped kale

Directions:

1. Place a soup pot over high heat. Add oil. When the oil is heated, add onion, celery, carrot and red pepper and sauté until tender.
2. Stir in the garlic and cook until aromatic.
3. Add cauliflower, spices and salt and sauté for a couple of minutes.
4. Add broth and stir. When it begins to boil, lower the heat and cook until cauliflower is tender.
5. Add chickpeas and kale and cook until kale wilts.
6. Add salt and pepper to taste.
7. Ladle into soup bowls and serve hot or warm.

Detox Breakfast Stew

Number of servings: 4

Nutritional values per serving:

Calories – 117, Fat – NA, Carbohydrate – 27 g, Fiber – NA, Protein – 2 g

Ingredients:

- 2 sweet potatoes, peeled, cubed
- 2 parsnips, peeled, chopped
- 6 cloves garlic, crushed
- Chili powder to taste
- 2 teaspoons ground cumin
- 4 cups vegetable broth, warmed
- 1 cup cooked red lentils
- 2 teaspoons coconut milk, to garnish
- 6 carrots, roughly chopped
- 2 onions, quartered
- ½ teaspoon sea salt
- 1 ½ teaspoon turmeric powder
- 2 tablespoons coconut oil
- 1 inch fresh ginger, peeled, grated
- A handful fresh parsley, chopped, to garnish

Directions:

1. Place a sheet of parchment paper over a large baking sheet.
2. Add all the vegetables, spices and coconut oil into a bowl. Toss well.
3. Spread onto the prepared baking sheet.
4. Bake in a preheated oven at 350° F for about 20 minutes or until charred lightly.

5. Remove from the oven and cool for a while. Add the vegetables into a blender.
6. Blend for 30-40 seconds or until smooth.
7. Add broth, lentils, ginger and blend until smooth.
8. Ladle into bowls. Drizzle coconut milk on top and serve.

Savory Saffron Kombu Congee

Number of servings: 4

Nutritional values per serving:

Calories – 215, Fat – NA, Carbohydrate – 51 g, Fiber – NA, Protein – 4 g

Ingredients:

- 1 cup long grain jasmine rice, rinsed, soaked in 3 cups water overnight
- 4 medium carrots, chopped
- 2 inches fresh ginger, grated
- 2 bunches arugula, chopped
- Sea salt to taste
- Olive oil, as required
- 3.5 ounces green beans, sliced
- 2 bunches fresh parsley, chopped
- 8-10 threads saffron
- 2 bunches chives, chopped
- 2 tablespoons minced lemongrass leaves
- 2 pieces kombu seaweed, cut into strips

Directions:

1. Add soaked rice along with water into a pot. Place the pot over low heat and cook until rice is soft and creamy.
2. Add saffron during the last 10 minutes of cooking. It will take a couple of hours. Stir occasionally initially and frequently towards the end.
3. Meanwhile, place a saucepan with water over high heat. Add salt and bring to a boil. Add green beans and cook for a minute. Drain and immerse in chilled water for a few minutes. Strain and set aside.

4. Place a wok over medium-high heat. Add oil. When the oil is heated, add ginger, a little salt and carrots and cook for about 3 minutes.
5. Stir in the lemongrass, arugula and green beans and cook for a couple of minutes. Turn off the heat and transfer into the simmering congee during the last 5 minutes of cooking.
6. Stir in chives and parsley. Turn off the heat.
7. Ladle into bowls and serve.

Lemony Coconut Lentil Soup

Number of servings: 3

Nutritional values per serving:

Calories – 161, Fat – 7 g, Carbohydrate – 19 g, Fiber – 7 g, Protein – 7 g

Ingredients:

- 1 tablespoon coconut oil
- 2 cloves garlic, minced
- 1 carrot, chopped
- 1 small yellow onion, minced
- 1 stalk celery, chopped
- ¾ teaspoon smoked paprika
- ¼ teaspoon ground coriander
- ¾ teaspoon ground cumin
- 2 cups water
- 2 cups vegetable broth
- 1 cup red lentils, rinsed, soaked in water for an hour
- 1 tablespoon fresh lemon juice or to taste
- Sea salt to taste
- Pepper to taste
- A handful fresh cilantro, chopped, to garnish (optional)
- 2 tablespoons tomato paste
- 3 tablespoons full-fat coconut milk
- Crushed red pepper flakes, to garnish

Directions:

1. Place a soup pot over medium flame. Add oil. When the oil is heated, add onion and cook until pink.
2. Stir in the garlic and cook until aromatic.
3. Add carrots, celery and spices and cook for 3-4 minutes.
4. Stir in the lentils, water, broth and tomato paste.

5. When the soup begins to boil, lower the heat and cover with a lid. Cook until the lentils are soft. It can take 30-50 minutes.
6. Add coconut milk, lemon juice, salt and pepper and stir.
7. Ladle into soup bowls. Sprinkle crushed red pepper flakes and cilantro on top and serve.

Vegetarian Breakfast Posole

Number of servings: 4

Nutritional values per serving:

Calories – 189, Fat – 9.5 g, Carbohydrate – 24.2 g, Fiber – 5.9 g, Protein – 5.1 g

Ingredients:

For posole:

- 1 ½ cups cooked or canned hominy, drained
- 1 ½ cups chopped Hatch green chilies
- 2 dried New Mexico chilies, chopped
- 2 cloves garlic, minced
- ½ tablespoon miso paste
- 1 small onion, chopped
- Salt to taste
- 6 cups vegetable stock
- 2 tablespoons chili powder
- 1-2 chipotle chili peppers in adobo sauce, chopped
- 1 medium ripe tomato, chopped
- ½ teaspoon oregano

To serve:

- 1 medium avocado, peeled, pitted, quartered
- Butter or Earth balance butter
- ¼ cup chopped fresh cilantro
- 4 large eggs – if you have no issues with eating eggs in a plant based diet

Directions:

1. Add all the ingredients for posole into a soup pot. Place the soup pot over medium heat.
2. When it begins to boil, lower the heat and simmer for 40-50 minutes. Stir occasionally.
3. To serve: Ladle into 4 soup bowls. Place 1 piece of avocado in each bowl.
4. Cook eggs in butter, sunny side up (if using eggs). Place an egg in each bowl and serve garnished with cilantro.

Chipotle Black Bean Tortilla Soup

Number of servings: 3

Nutritional values per serving:

Calories – 265, Fat –5.3 g, Carbohydrate – 51 g, Fiber – 10.6 g, Protein – 11.6 g

Ingredients:

- 1 tablespoon avocado oil or coconut oil
- 2 cloves garlic, minced
- ¾ teaspoon ground cumin
- ¾ cup red chipotle salsa or any other spicy salsa
- 1 tablespoon coconut sugar or maple syrup
- ½ can (from a 15.25 ounces can) whole corn kernels (drained)
- 1 small onion, chopped
- ¼ red or orange bell pepper, diced
- ½ teaspoon chili powder
- 2 cups vegetable stock
- 1 can (15 ounces) black beans, drain some of its liquid

To serve; Optional

- Lime juice to taste
- A handful tortilla chips
- A handful fresh cilantro, chopped
- 1 small red onion, chopped
- 1 small ripe avocado, peeled, cubed
- Hot sauce to taste

Directions:

1. Place a soup pot over medium flame. Add oil. When the oil is heated, add onion, garlic and pepper and sauté for a minute. Season with salt and pepper.
2. Cook until the vegetables are tender.
3. Stir in cumin and chili powder. Cook for a few seconds until aromatic.
4. Stir in salsa, sugar and stock. Raise the heat to medium-high heat. When it begins to boil, stir in corn and black beans.
5. Lower the heat to low heat and cook for 20-30 minutes. Stir occasionally.
6. Ladle into soup bowls and serve with suggested serving options if desired.

Chapter Fifteen: Plant Based Breakfast Salad Recipes

Baby Kale Breakfast Salad with Quinoa & Strawberries

Number of servings: 2

Nutritional values per serving:

Calories – 330, Fat – 20 g, Carbohydrate – 31 g, Fiber – 6 g, Protein – 9 g

Ingredients:

- 2 teaspoons minced garlic
- 2 tablespoons extra-virgin olive oil
- Pepper to taste
- 1 cup cooked quinoa
- 2 tablespoons salted pepitas
- Salt to taste
- 4 teaspoons red wine vinegar
- 6 cups lightly packed baby kale
- 1 cup strawberry slices

Directions:

1. Place garlic and salt in a bowl. Using a fork or back of a spoon, mash the salt and garlic into a paste.
2. Add garlic paste, vinegar, oil and pepper into a bowl and whisk well.
3. Stir in the kale.
4. Divide kale into 2 bowls. Place quinoa over the kale.
5. Sprinkle strawberries and pepitas on top and serve.

Pomegranate-Farro Breakfast Salad with Honey Ricotta

Number of servings: 2

Nutritional values per serving:

Calories – 294, Fat – 13.3 g, Carbohydrate – 41 g, Fiber – 8 g, Protein – 12 g

Ingredients:

- 6 tablespoons part-skim ricotta cheese
- 1 teaspoon honey
- 2 teaspoons fresh lemon juice or tangerine juice
- 4 cups fresh baby spinach
- 2/3 cup pomegranate arils
- 1 teaspoon grated lemon or tangerine zest
- 2 teaspoon extra-virgin olive oil
- Salt to taste
- 2/3 cup cooked whole grain farro
- 2 tablespoons roasted, chopped almonds

Directions:

1. Add ricotta, lemon zest and honey into a bowl and stir.
2. Add oil, zest and salt into another bowl and whisk well. Add spinach and farro and toss.
3. Divide the spinach mixture into 2 shallow bowls.
4. Sprinkle pomegranate arils over the spinach layer.
5. Spread ricotta mixture on top of the pomegranate. Sprinkle almonds on top and serve.

Coronation Chickpea and Apple Salad

Number of servings: 2

Nutritional values per serving:

Calories – 223, Fat – 6.2 g, Carbohydrate – 30 g, Fiber – 6.4 g, Protein – 8.6 g

Ingredients:

For salad:

- 2 spring onions, chopped
- 1 green apple, cored, diced
- ½ can (from a 14.2 ounces can) chickpeas, rinsed, drained
- 1 little gems lettuce, separate the leaves
- 1 stick celery, sliced diagonally
- 1 tablespoon golden raisins
- ½ cup chopped fresh cilantro + extra to garnish

For dressing:

- 1 teaspoon curry paste
- 1 ½ tablespoons Greek yogurt
- 1 tablespoon mango chutney
- Juice of ½ lime

Directions:

1. Add all the ingredients for dressing into a bowl and whisk well. Set aside for a while for the flavors to set in.
2. Divide and place lettuce leaves on 2 serving plates.
3. Add remaining salad ingredients into a bowl and toss well.
4. Drizzle dressing over the salad and toss well. Place over the lettuce leaves.

5. Garnish with cilantro leaves and serve.

Barley Salad with Tomatoes, Cucumber and Parsley

Number of servings: 4

Nutritional values per serving:

Calories – 154, Fat – 7 g, Carbohydrate – 20 g, Fiber – 5 g, Protein – 4 g

Ingredients:

For salad:

- ½ cup uncooked pearly barley
- ½ English cucumber, diced
- 1 tomato, deseeded, diced
- ¼ cup chopped flat leaf parsley

For dressing:

- 1 ½ tablespoons fresh lemon juice
- Salt to taste
- Pepper to taste
- 2 tablespoons extra-virgin olive oil
- ½ teaspoon za'tar (optional)

Directions:

1. Follow the instructions on the package and cook the pearl barley. When cooked, fluff with a fork.
2. Transfer into a bowl. Add rest of the salad ingredients and toss well.
3. Add all the ingredients for dressing into a bowl and whisk well. Pour over the salad.
4. Toss well and serve.

Three-Bean Salad

Number of servings: 4

Nutritional values per serving:

Calories – 193, Fat – 2 g, Carbohydrate – 37 g, Fiber – 8 g, Protein – 9 g

Ingredients:

For dressing:

- 1 ½ tablespoons cider vinegar
- ½ tablespoon sugar
- ½ tablespoon canola oil
- 1 ½ tablespoons rice vinegar
- ½ tablespoon whole-grain mustard
- ¼ teaspoon salt or to taste
- Freshly ground pepper, to taste

For salad:

- 3 tablespoons diced red onion
- ½ package (from a 10 ounces package) frozen baby lima beans, or shelled edamame
- 1 tablespoon chopped fresh parsley
- ½ can (from a 15 ounces can) black-eyed peas or chickpeas, rinsed
- ½ pound green beans, trimmed and cut into 1-inch pieces

Directions:

1. To make dressing: Add all the ingredients for dressing into a large bowl and whisk well.
2. Add onion and black-eyed peas and toss well. Set aside

3. Place a saucepan with water over high heat. When it begins to boil, add lima beans and cook until tender. Take out the beans with a slotted spoon and immerse in ice water for a few minutes. Drain and dry by patting with a kitchen towel. Place in the bowl of dressing.
4. Add green beans into the simmering water in the saucepan and cook for about 3 minutes. Drain off the water and immerse in ice water for a few minutes.
5. Drain and dry with a kitchen towel. Add into the bowl of dressing and toss well.
6. Cover and set aside for a few minutes for the flavors to set in.
7. Divide into 4 portions and serve.

Chapter Sixteen: Plant Based Breakfast Recipes with Fruits

Whole Grain Peanut Butter and Fruit Toast

Number of servings: 1

Nutritional values per serving:

Calories – 382, Fat – 28 g, Carbohydrate – 30 g, Fiber – 5 g, Protein – 6 g

Ingredients:

- 1 slice whole grain bread, toasted
- ½ small banana, sliced
- 1 tablespoon sliced almonds
- 2 tablespoons peanut butter
- 1 large strawberry, sliced
- ½ teaspoon raw honey or agave nectar

Directions:

1. Smear peanut butter over the bread slice.
2. Place a layer of banana followed by a layer of strawberries.
3. Place any remaining banana or strawberry slices.
4. Scatter almonds on top.
5. Trickle honey on top and serve.

Morning Banana Split

Number of servings: 2

Nutritional values per serving:

Calories – 340, Fat – 14 g, Carbohydrate – 48 g, Fiber – 6 g, Protein – 15 g

Ingredients:

- 2 bananas, halved lengthwise
- 2 teaspoons cocoa powder
- ½ cup sliced fresh strawberries
- 2 tablespoons chopped, roasted peanuts
- 1 cup plain Greek yogurt, divided
- 2 teaspoons honey
- ½ cup crushed fresh pineapple

Directions:

1. Place 2 banana halves in each of 2 wide shallow bowls, with the cut side facing up.
2. Set aside 2 tablespoons of yogurt and drizzle the remaining yogurt over the cut part of the banana.
3. Add the retained yogurt, cocoa and honey into a bowl and whisk well. Add strawberries, peanuts and pineapple and stir until well coated.
4. Scatter the strawberry mixture over the bananas and serve.

Pineapple and Berry Salad

Number of servings: 4

Nutritional values per serving:

Calories – 55, Fat – 0 g, Carbohydrate – 14 g, Fiber – 3 g, Protein – 1 g

Ingredients:

- 1 fresh pineapple, peeled, cubed
- ½ pound strawberries, hulled, sliced
- ½ cup blackberries, halved
- ½ kiwi, peeled, sliced

Directions:

1. Add all the ingredients into a bowl and toss well.
2. Divide into plates and serve.

Grapefruit, Agave & Pistachio Salad

Number of servings: 4

Nutritional values per serving:

Calories – 107, Fat – 1 g, Carbohydrate – 21 g, Fiber – 2 g, Protein – 2 g

Ingredients:

- 2 white grapefruits, peeled, separated into segments, deseeded, chopped
- 2 pink grapefruits, peeled, separated into segments, deseeded, chopped
- 2 teaspoons chopped pistachio nuts
- 2 tablespoons agave nectar

Directions:

1. Add the grapefruits into a bowl and toss.
2. Divide into 4 bowls. Sprinkle ½ teaspoon pistachio nuts in each bowl.
3. Drizzle ½ tablespoon agave nectar on top and serve.

Fruit Punch

Number of servings: 2

Nutritional values per serving:

Calories – 69, Fat – 0.4 g, Carbohydrate – 17.2 g, Fiber – 1.9 g, Protein – 0.8 g

Ingredients:

- ½ cup halved green grapes
- 1 small peach, pitted, chopped
- 4 fresh strawberries, hulled, chopped
- 1/3 cup fresh blueberries
- 3 tablespoons fresh orange juice
- ¼ Granny Smith apple, chopped

Directions:

1. Add all the ingredients into a bowl and toss well.
2. Divide into 2 bowls and serve.

Papaya Boat Parfait

Number of servings: 4

Nutritional values per serving:

Calories – 313, Fat – 12 g, Carbohydrate – 43 g, Fiber – 6 g, Protein – 13 g

Ingredients:

- 2 whole papayas, halved lengthwise, deseeded
- 4 teaspoons honey or agave nectar
- 2 kiwis, peeled, chopped
- 4 tablespoons slivered almonds
- 2 cups plain Greek yogurt or nondairy yogurt of your choice
- 4 tablespoons pomegranate seeds
- 1 teaspoon chia seeds

Directions:

1. Do not peel the papayas. Scoop out some of the pulp from the papaya halves to resemble boats.
2. Divide the yogurt among the papaya boats. Drizzle a teaspoon of honey over the yogurt in each bowl.
3. Sprinkle rest of the ingredients in the boats and serve.

Healthy Breakfast Fruit Pizza

Number of servings: 4

Nutritional values per serving:

Calories – 194, Fat – 2 g, Carbohydrate – 37 g, Fiber – 3 g, Protein – 4 g

Ingredients:

- 1 flax egg (1 tablespoon ground flaxseeds mixed with 3 tablespoons water)
- ¼ cup pure maple syrup
- 1 ½ cups gluten-free rolled oats
- ½ tablespoon ground cinnamon
- 3 tablespoons unsweetened apple sauce
- ½ teaspoon vanilla extract
- ¼ teaspoon sea salt
- ½ cup mixed fruit (mixture of berries and kiwi)

For coconut whipped cream:

- 1 can (14 ounces can) full fat very chilled coconut milk
- ¼ teaspoon vanilla extract
- 2 tablespoons powdered sugar
- A small pinch salt

Directions:

1. For crust: Grease a 6-inch pie pan or springform pan with cooking spray.
2. Line the pan with parchment paper.
3. After making the flax egg, refrigerate for 15 minutes.
4. Add all the dry ingredients into a mixing bowl and stir.
5. Add all the wet ingredients except fruits into another bowl and whisk well.

6. Pour wet ingredients into the bowl of dry ingredients and mix until well incorporated.
7. Transfer the mixture onto the prepared pie pan. Press it well onto the bottom of the pan.
8. Bake in a preheated oven at 375° F for about 10-12 minutes or until light brown.
9. Remove the pan from the oven and cool for 15 minutes in the pan. Remove the crust from the pan and place on a wire rack. Let it cool to room temperature.
10. Meanwhile, make the coconut whipped cream as follows: Firstly chill a can of coconut milk for 8-10 hours. Cut open the can and scoop out half the coconut cream that is floating on top and place in a chilled bowl. Use the remaining coconut cream with liquid in some other recipe.
11. Also chill the beaters of the hand mixer. Beat the coconut cream until creamy.
12. Whip in the sugar, vanilla and salt.
13. Place the bowl in the freezer for 10 minutes.
14. Spread the coconut cream on the cooled crust. Scatter fruits all over the crust.
15. Cut into 4 wedges and serve.

Summertime Fruit Salad

Number of servings: 3

Nutritional values per serving:

Calories – 91, Fat – 0.6 22.4 g, Carbohydrate – 22.4 g, Fiber – 4 g, Protein – 1.7 g

Ingredients:

- ½ pound strawberries, hulled, thinly sliced
- ½ cup blueberries
- 1 tablespoon lemon juice
- 1 teaspoon balsamic vinegar
- 3 small peaches, thinly sliced
- A handful basil or mint, chopped
- ½ tablespoon maple syrup or honey

Directions:

1. Add all the fruits into a bowl and toss well.
2. Add rest of the ingredients into a bowl and whisk well.
3. Pour over the fruits. Toss lightly.
4. Serve at room temperature for refrigerate for a few hours and serve chilled.

Blueberry-Pineapple Salad with Creamy Yogurt Dressing

Number of servings: 2

Nutritional values per serving:

Calories – 123, Fat – 1.2 g, Carbohydrate – 29.2 g, Fiber – 2 g, Protein – 1.4 g

Ingredients:

- ½ can (from a 10 ounces can) pineapple chunks in juice, retain some of the juice
- ½ teaspoon honey or to taste
- ½ cup fresh blueberries
- 1 ½ tablespoons whole milk plain Greek yogurt
- 1/8 teaspoon grated lime zest

Directions:

1. Add ½ tablespoon pineapple juice, honey, yogurt and lime zest into a bowl and whisk well.
2. Add rest of the ingredients and fold gently.
3. Divide into 2 bowls and serve.

Fresh Fruit Medley

Number of servings: 4

Nutritional values per serving:

Calories – 156, Fat – 0.9 g, Carbohydrate – 38.1 g, Fiber – 6.3 g, Protein – 2.6 g

Ingredients:

- 2 small oranges, peeled, separated into segments, chopped
- 1 cup fresh blueberries
- 1 cup fresh raspberries
- 1 cup sliced fresh strawberries
- 1 small banana, sliced
- 1 mango, peeled, deseeded, cubed
- 2 tablespoon maple syrup (optional)
- 4 tablespoons plain yogurt
- 1 teaspoon white sugar

Directions:

1. Add oranges, strawberries, blueberries, raspberries and banana into a large bowl and toss well.
2. Add yogurt, sugar and maple syrup and stir until well incorporated.
3. Divide into bowls and serve.

Chapter Seventeen: Plant Based Breakfast Bar and Bites Recipes

Chocolate Peanut Butter Oatmeal Bars

Number of servings: 6

Nutritional values per serving: 1 bar

Calories – 217, Fat – 15 g, Carbohydrate – 17 g, Fiber – 4 g, Protein – 7 g

Ingredients:

- 1 cup rolled oats
- ¼ cup overripe mashed banana
- 2 tablespoons almond flour or meal
- 1 tablespoon ground flaxseeds
- ½ scoop vanilla or chocolate plant based protein powder
- 1 cup coconut milk

- 2 tablespoons peanut butter, unsweetened
- 2 tablespoons cocoa powder
- 2 tablespoons chopped peanuts

Directions:

1. Grease a small baking dish (6-7 inches) with cooking spray.
2. Add all the ingredients into a bowl and stir until just incorporated.
3. Transfer into the prepared baking dish. Press it well onto the bottom of the dish.
4. Bake in a preheated oven at 350° F for about 20 minutes or until slightly hard on top.
5. Cut into 6 equal slices and serve either hot or at room temperature.

Cheesecake Breakfast Bars

Number of servings: 4

Nutritional values per serving: 1 bar

Calories – 127, Fat – 9.8 g, Carbohydrate – 9.5 g, Fiber – 8 g, Protein – 7 g

Ingredients:

- 2 ounces cream cheese, softened
- ¼ cup canned coconut milk (shake the can well before pouring)
- 1 scoop vanilla whey protein powder or any plant based protein powder
- ½ teaspoon ground cinnamon to sprinkle
- 1 tablespoon butter, softened
- 2 tablespoons swerve or any other granulated sweetener of your choice
- 1 tablespoon coconut flour

Directions:

1. Add cream cheese, butter and swerve into a mixing bowl. Beat with an electric hand mixer until creamy.
2. Add coconut milk and mix well. Add coconut flour and protein powder and mix well.
3. Transfer into a small greased baking dish. Spread it evenly. Sprinkle cinnamon over it.
4. Bake in a preheated oven at 350° F for about 20 minutes or until set.
5. Remove from the oven and cool to room temperature.
6. Cut into 4 equal slices and serve.

Strawberry Rhubarb Buckwheat Bars

Number of servings: 12

Nutritional values per serving: 1 bar

Calories – 186, Fat – 8 g, Carbohydrate – 30 g, Fiber – 2 g, Protein – 3 g

Ingredients:

For crust:

- 1 ¼ cups whole wheat flour
- ¼ cup coconut sugar
- ½ teaspoon baking powder
- 1 small flax egg (½ tablespoon flaxseed meal mixed with 1 ½ tablespoons water)
- 1 ½ tablespoons molasses
- 6 tablespoons buckwheat flour
- ½ teaspoon kosher salt
- ½ cup cold butter, unsalted, chopped into small cubes
- 1 tablespoon honey or agave nectar

For filling:

- 1 cup strawberries, hulled
- ½ jar (from a 12 ounces jar) no-sugar added strawberry preserves
- 1 teaspoon lemon juice
- 1 cup chopped rhubarb
- ½ tablespoon cornstarch

Directions:

1. Set aside the flax egg for 15 minutes in the refrigerator, after mixing flaxseed meal and water.

2. To make crust: Add all the dry ingredients into the food processor bowl and process until well incorporated.
3. Scatter the butter cubes and give a few short pulses (of about 5-6 seconds each) until crumbs are formed.
4. Add rest of the ingredients for crust and pulse until well incorporated.
5. Set aside ¼ cup of the crust mixture and add rest of the mixture into a small rectangular baking dish (about 8 inches).
6. Press the mixture onto the bottom as well as a little on the sides of the baking dish.
7. Bake in a preheated oven at 375° F for about 10-15 minutes or until set.
8. Remove from the oven and cool to room temperature.
9. Meanwhile, make the filling as follows: Add all the ingredients for filling into the food processor bowl and give short pulses of 3-4 seconds until just incorporated. Do not blend the mixture until smooth. It should be chunky.
10. Transfer into a saucepan. Place the saucepan over medium heat. Simmer until thick.
11. Spoon the mixture over the crust. Sprinkle ¼ cup crumbs (that was set aside) on top.
12. Bake for another 15-20 minutes or until the top is light brown.
13. Remove from the oven and cool to room temperature.
14. Cut into 12 equal slices and serve.

Peanut Butter Breakfast Bar

Number of servings: 4

Nutritional values per serving: 1 bar

Calories – 232, Fat – 9 g, Carbohydrate – 39 g, Fiber – 4 g, Protein – 5 g

Ingredients:

- ¾ cup dates, pitted
- ¼ cup old fashioned oats
- ¼ cup peanut butter, unsweetened

Directions:

1. If your dates are very dry, soak in warm water 20 to 30 minutes. Add dates into the food processor bowl and pulse until chopped into smaller pieces.
2. Add oats and peanut butter and give short pulses until just incorporated. Do not over-process.
3. Transfer into a lined baking dish. Spread it evenly.
4. Freeze until slightly firm.
5. Cut into 4 slices and serve.

Apricot Oats Protein Bars

Number of servings: 5

Nutritional values per serving: 1 bar

Calories – 232, Fat – 11.3 g, Carbohydrate – 23.8 g, Fiber – 5.1 g, Protein – 13.2 g

Ingredients:

- ¾ cup pumpkin seeds
- ¼ cup flax seeds
- ½ cup gluten-free rolled oats
- ½ cup dried Turkish apricots + extra to garnish
- Hot water, as required
- 2 tablespoons maple syrup or honey
- A pinch salt
- ¼ teaspoon ground cinnamon
- ¼ cup plant based vanilla protein powder

Directions:

1. Place a sheet of parchment paper on the bottom of a square-baking dish (6 x6).
2. Place pumpkin seeds, flax seeds and oats in a blender or food processor and blend until finely powdered.
3. Transfer into a bowl.
4. Add apricots into the blender or food processor and process until finely chopped.
5. Transfer into the bowl of oats mixture.
6. Add protein powder, cinnamon and salt and mix until well combined.
7. Add about 3 tablespoons water, maple syrup and vanilla into another bowl and whisk well.

8. Pour into the bowl of dry ingredients. Mix until well incorporated. You may need to use your hands while mixing.
9. Spoon the mixture into the prepared baking dish.
10. Chill for an hour or until it sets.
11. Cut into 5 equal slices and serve. Leftovers should be refrigerated until use.

Cranberry Blueberry Crumb Bars

Number of servings: 12

Nutritional values per serving: 1 bar

Calories – 211, Fat – 8 g, Carbohydrate – 32 g, Fiber – 4 g, Protein – 4 g

Ingredients:

For cranberry – blueberry layer:

- 1 cup cranberries, fresh or frozen
- ½ cup blueberries, fresh or frozen
- 4 tablespoons raw sugar
- 2 teaspoons chia seeds
- 4 teaspoons lime juice
- 6 tablespoons water

For crust:

- 1 ½ cups whole wheat flour
- ½ cup almond flour
- ½ teaspoon salt
- 1 ½ cups old fashioned oats
- ½ teaspoon baking soda
- ½ cup ground, raw sugar
- 1 teaspoon ground cinnamon
- 4 tablespoons solid coconut oil
- 2 teaspoons vanilla extract
- 2 teaspoons lime juice
- 4 tablespoons almond milk or more if required

Directions:

1. For cranberry-blueberry layer: Add all the ingredients for cranberry-blueberry layer into a saucepan.

2. Place the saucepan over medium heat. Cook until the berries are broken down. Turn off the heat. Mash half the berries with the back of a spoon.
3. To make crust: Add all the ingredients except milk into a bowl and mix until well incorporated.
4. Drizzle milk over it and mix until crumbs are formed.
5. Set aside ¼ of the crust mixture aside.
6. Add rest of the crust mixture into a baking pan lined with parchment paper. Press it well onto the bottom of the pan.
7. Spoon the blueberry-cranberry mixture over the crust.
8. Sprinkle the retained crust mixture on top. Spray some cooking spray over the top crust.
9. Bake in a preheated oven at 350° F for about 25-30 minutes or until golden brown on top.
10. Take out the dish from the oven and cool to room temperature.
11. Cut into 12 equal slices.
12. Store leftovers in an airtight container in the refrigerator for 4-5 days.

Black Bean Brownie Bites

Number of servings: 6

Nutritional values per serving: 1 bite

Calories – 149, Fat – 4.9 g, Carbohydrate – 24.8 g, Fiber – 5.2 g, Protein – 5.9 g

Ingredients:

- 1 tablespoon flaxseed meal
- ½ cup cooked or canned black beans, rinsed, drained
- ¼ cup almond meal
- ½ teaspoon vanilla extract
- ¾ teaspoon baking powder
- 1 tablespoon chopped pecans
- 3 tablespoons water
- 6 tablespoons cocoa powder, unsweetened
- ¼ teaspoon sea salt
- ¼ cup organic sugar
- 1 tablespoon dairy-free chocolate chips

Directions:

1. Grease a 6 counts muffin pan with cooking spray. Place disposable liners in it.
2. Make flax egg my mixing flaxseed meal and water. Refrigerate for 15 minutes.
3. Add flax egg, black beans and all the dry ingredients into the food processor bowl.
4. Spoon the batter into the prepared baking pan. Fill up to half the cups.
5. Sprinkle pecans and chocolate chips. Press lightly into the batter.
6. Bake in a preheated oven at 350° F for about 20 minutes or until set.

7. Remove from the oven and cool to room temperature.
8. Remove from the muffin cups and serve.

Key Lime Pie Energy Bites

Number of servings: 5

Nutritional values per serving: 1 ball

Calories – 123, Fat – 7 g, Carbohydrate – 14 g, Fiber – 2 g, Protein – 2 g

Ingredients:

- ¼ cup raw almonds
- 2 tablespoons walnuts or pecans
- Zest of ½ lime + a little extra to garnish
- A pinch salt
- ½ cup pitted dates
- 3 tablespoons shredded, unsweetened coconut + extra to dredge
- 2-3 tablespoons lime juice

Directions:

1. Place almonds into the food processor bowl and process for 5-6 seconds until roughly chopped.
2. Add rest of the ingredients and process until well combined and the preferred texture (like smooth or chunky). Transfer into a bowl.
3. If the mixture is sticky, grease your hands with a little oil.
4. Divide the mixture into 5 portions and shape into balls.
5. Add some shredded coconut and a little lime zest in a bowl and stir.
6. Dredge in shredded coconut mixture and serve.

Banana-Oat Protein Balls

Number of servings: 24

Nutritional values per serving: 1 ball

Calories – 47, Fat – 0.7 g, Carbohydrate – 8 g, Fiber – 1.2 g, Protein – 2.7 g

Ingredients:

- 2 scoops vegan vanilla protein powder
- 2 cups rolled oats
- 2 large bananas, sliced

Directions:

1. Add oats and protein powder into the food processor bowl. Pulse for 5-6 seconds until chopped into pieces but not finely powdered.
2. Add banana and pulse until well combined.
3. Transfer into a bowl.
4. Divide the mixture into 24 equal portions and shape into balls.
5. Place in an airtight container in the refrigerator for 4-5 days.

Conclusion

As you come to the end of this book, I would first like to thank you for purchasing it and investing your time in reading through it. I hope you found it informative and useful. By now, you know enough about the plant-based diet to understand why it is recommended and how it can help you.

The recipes given in this book will help you cook up some delicious breakfasts every single day. Not only will the food be delicious, but you will also have the satisfaction of knowing that you are starting your day with a healthy meal. All of the recipes are completely plant-based and will help you lose weight in a healthy way. You can try new recipes and switch up ingredients to suit your taste as well.

To begin with, try out all the different recipes and work your way through them. You will soon see how appealing and amazing the plant-based diet is. This diet will not just help you be more health-conscious but also more humane towards animals. Once you try out these yummy recipes, you'll be sold on the diet and recommend it to everyone else you know as well.

Watch out for my next book in this series which will cover delicious and easy meal recipes and after that dessert recipes. Thank you so much for reading and let me know what you think of my recipes! Even better, if you have suggestions to improve them or have one of your own, let me know!

Happy eating!

Made in the USA
Coppell, TX
25 October 2019